TIME PASSAGES

By Robert Burtt & Bill Main

"The key to unlocking the door to our future
opens with a journey into the past."

Robert Burtt & Bill Main

FIRST PRINTING

Global millennium celebrations proceed as the fears of Y2K mayhem disappear.

Sunday	Monday	Tuesday	Wednesday	Thursday	Friday	Saturday

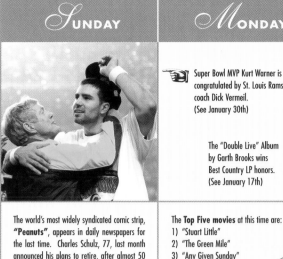

Week 1

Monday: Super Bowl MVP Kurt Warner is congratulated by St. Louis Rams coach Dick Vermeil. (See January 30th)

The "Double Live" Album by Garth Brooks wins Best Country LP honors. (See January 17th)

Wednesday: Cartoonist Charles Schulz retires from drawing his daily "Peanuts" comic strip. (See January 2nd)

Saturday 1: **Millennium celebrations take place around the world** including Barbra Streisand's New Year's Eve show at the MGM Grand in Las Vegas which grosses a record $14.7 million for a single concert.

Wisconsin, led by Heisman trophy winner Ron Dayne, becomes the first big ten team to win consecutive Rose Bowls, defeating Stanford 17-9. Cotton Bowl: Arkansas 27 - Texas 6. Outback Bowl: Georgia 28 - Purdue 25 in overtime.

---

2 (Sunday): The world's most widely syndicated comic strip, "Peanuts", appears in daily newspapers for the last time. Charles Schulz, 77, last month announced his plans to retire, after almost 50 years, to concentrate on his treatment for colon cancer.

Fiesta Bowl: Nebraska 31 - Tennessee 21
Orange Bowl: Michigan 35 - Alabama 34 in overtime.

3 (Monday): The **Top Five movies** at this time are:
1) "Stuart Little"
2) "The Green Mile"
3) "Any Given Sunday"
4) "Toy Story 2"
5) "The Talented Mr. Ripley"

The #1 song on the Billboard Hot Country Singles Music Chart is "Breathe" by Faith Hill.

4 (Tuesday): Broadcasting mogul **Ted Turner**, 61, and actress **Jane Fonda**, 62, announce that they are separating, but will stay married. The couple, who married December 21st, 1991, say they need personal time apart.

The **Florida State Seminoles** win the NCAA Division 1-A football championship with a 49-29 victory over Virginia Tech, in the Sugar Bowl in New Orleans.

5 (Wednesday): The U.S. Immigration & Naturalization Service orders the Florida relatives of **Elian Gonzalez**, 6, return the boy to his father in Cuba by January 14th. The boy was rescued in the Atlantic Ocean off southern Florida on November 25th, 1999, after drifting for two days on an inner tube. His mother and stepfather drowned with ten others after fleeing Cuba seeking refuge in the United States.

6 (Thursday): The Rolling Stones' "(I Can't Get No) Satisfaction" tops the VH1 poll of 700 people in the music industry for the **top 100 greatest rock songs**. The #2 song selected is "Respect" by Aretha Franklin and #3 is "Stairway to Heaven" by Led Zeppelin.

"Mad Magazine" cartoonist, **Don Martin**, 68, dies of cancer in Miami, Florida.

7 (Friday): **Chart Toppers:** The #1 song on the Billboard Hot 100 Singles Music Chart is "Smooth" by Santana featuring Rob Thomas.

The #1 album on the Billboard 200 Music Chart is "All The Way....A Decade of Song" by Celine Dion.

8 (Saturday): CBS-TV premieres the new game show "Winning Lines", hosted by Dick Clark.

NFL Wildcard Games:
AFC: Tennessee 22 - Buffalo 16
NFC: Washington 27 - Detroit 13

---

9 (Sunday): **NFL Wildcard Games:**
NFC: Dallas 10 - Minnesota 27
AFC: Miami 20 - Seattle 17

NBC-TV premieres the new game show "Twenty One", hosted by Maury Povich.

10 (Monday): Kapalua, Hawaii: **Tiger Woods** wins the PGA season opener at the Mercedes Championship, in a play-off with Ernie Els. This is Woods' 5th consecutive victory and the longest winning streak in 46 years, since Ben Hogan won five consecutive events in 1953.

Claudia Shear's comedy play, "Dirty Blonde", opens at the New York Theater Workshop. It will move to the Helen Hayes Theater on May 1st.
BROADWAY

11 (Tuesday): Former catcher Carlton Fisk and first baseman Tony Perez are elected to the **Baseball Hall of Fame** in Cooperstown, New York. Former manager Sparky Anderson will be elected in by the Veteran's Committee on February 29th.

Heir to the pharmaceuticals firm Johnson & Johnson, **Robert Wood Johnson IV**, is approved to buy the NFL NY Jets for $635 million.

12 (Wednesday): NBA Hornet point guard **Bobby Phills**, 30, is killed in a three-vehicle car crash in Charlotte, N.C.

First Lady **Hillary Rodham Clinton** appears on "The Late Show with David Letterman".

U.S. Attorney General **Janet Reno** upholds a decison giving custody of Elian Gonzalez, 6, to his Cuban father.

13 (Thursday): **Sean "Puffy" Combs**, 30, is indicted on charges of criminal possession of two stolen guns found in his sport utility vehicle as he fled a Times Square night club shooting on December 27th, 1999. Combs was taken into custody, along with girlfriend Jennifer Lopez, as they allegedly drove away from the scene of the shooting.

14 (Friday): The hit TV show "The Simpsons" turns 10 years old today. On the February 13th episode, one of Springfield's own, Maude Flanders, will meet a tragic end.

"Late Show" host **David Letterman**, 52, undergoes emergency quintuple-bypass surgery at N.Y. Presbyterian Hospital.

15 (Saturday): A U.S. tourist is injured when a car smashes into the gates of British Prime Minister **Tony Blair's** official Downing Street residence. Blair was not home at the time. The woman suffered broken legs and her three sons were unharmed when pushed to safety.

NFL Play-off Games:
NFC: TB 14, Washington 13
AFC: Jacksonville 62 - Miami 7

---

16 (Sunday): Less than 24 hours after the worst defeat in Miami football franchise history, coach **Jimmy Johnson** retires from coaching after four seasons at Miami.
NFL Play-off Games:
NFC: St. Louis 49, Minnesota 37
AFC: Tennessee 19, Indianapolis 16
1999 LPGA "Player of the Year", Australian **Karrie Webb** wins the season-opening women's golf event in the Office Depot Tournament held at West Palm Beach, Florida.

17 (Monday): At the **American Music Awards** in L.A., Carlos Santana, 52, wins *Best LP* honors for "Supernatural". Brooks & Dunn win for *Favorite Country Band, Duo or Group*. Montgomery Gentry are named *Best New Country Artist*. Garth Brooks wins *Best Country LP* for "Double Live". Britney Spears wins *New Pop-Rock Artist*. Backstreet Boys win *Favorite Pop-Rock Band Award* and Shania Twain wins *Favorite Country Artist*.

18 (Tuesday): Canadian-born actor, **Michael J. Fox**, 38, announces his plans to leave the hit TV show "Spin City" at the end of this season. Fox, who has been diagnosed as having Parkinson's disease, plans to spend more time with his family (actress Tracy Pollan and their three children).

19 (Wednesday): Exotic film actress of the 1930's & 1940's, **Hedy Lamarr**, 86, is found dead at her home in Casselberry, Florida. The Austrian-born actress made her American film debut in "Algiers" (1938), co-starring Charles Boyer.

Former NBA great Michael Jordan becomes part-owner and president of basketball operations for the Washington Wizards.

20 (Thursday): **TV Programs Tonight on NBC:**
8:00 Friends
8:30 Jesse
9:00 Frasier
9:30 Stark Raving Mad
10:00 ER

TV Programs Tonight on CBS:
8:00 Diagnosis Murder
9:00 Chicago Hope
10:00 48 Hours

21 (Friday): The 220-lb, 4-feet-tall, personal robot "Tmsuk IV" is introduced to the Japanese consumer market. Costing approximately $70,000, the remote-controlled robot performs back massages and runs errands.

Miramax releases the romantic comedy film "Down To You", starring Freddie Prinze Jr. and Julia Stiles.

22 (Saturday): Emily Watson, Robert Carlyle and Ciaran Owens star in the film version of Frank McCourt's best-selling novel, "Angela's Ashes". The film is released by Paramount Pictures.

Antonio Banderas and Woody Harrelson set out to Las Vegas to fight each other, in the new comedy film "Play It To The Bone". Written & directed by Ron Shelton, the movie is released by Buena Vista.

---

23 (Sunday): **NFL Championship Games:**
NFC: St. Louis 11 - Tampa Bay 6
AFC: Tennessee 33 - Jacksonville 14
Tennessee QB **Steve McNair** completes 14 of 23 for 112 yards, 1 TD, and scores two more on one-yard QB keepers. He also has 9 carries for a team-high 91 yards.

24 (Monday): Veteran performers **Crosby, Stills, Nash and Young** kick off a 37-date North American tour at the Palace in Auburn Hills, Michigan. CSN formed in Los Angeles in 1968, with Neil Young joining a year later.

The revival of Eugene O'Neill's last completed play, "A Moon for the Misbegotten", opens at the Goodman Theatre in Chicago.
BROADWAY

25 (Tuesday): Tennis great **Martina Navratilova** is named to the Tennis Hall of Fame. During her career (1973-94), Navratilova won a record 167 singles and 165 doubles titles.

The #1 song on the Billboard Hot Country Singles Music Chart for the 4th consecutive week is "Breathe" by Faith Hill.

26 (Wednesday): **Chart Toppers:** The #1 song on the Billboard Hot 100 Singles Music Chart for the 2nd consecutive week is "What A Girl Wants" by Christina Aguilera.

Believed to be the **world's largest slot machine jackpot**, $34,955,489 U.S. is won by an unidentified woman in Las Vegas.

27 (Thursday): A record **snowstorm** hits North Carolina and the U.S. eastern seaboard. Many remain without electricity in the Carolinas, Florida and Texas.

President Bill Clinton delivers his final **State of the Union** address to a joint session of Congress. He proposes a $350 billion tax cut along with increased spending for schools and health care.

28 (Friday): The **Best-Selling Mass-Market Paperbacks** at this time are:
1) "The Testament" by John Grisham
2) "Angela's Ashes" by Frank McCourt
3) "The Green Mile" by Stephen King
4) "Dr. Atkins' New Diet Revolution" by Robert C. Atkins, M.D.
5) "The Carbohydrate Addict's Diet" by Dr. Richard Heller and Dr. Rachael Heller

29 (Saturday): American Lindsay Davenport wins the Women's Singles title at the **Australian Open** with a 6-1, 7-5 victory over Martina Hingis. Top-seeded Lisa Raymond (USA) and Rennae Stubbs of Australia win the doubles crown, defeating Hingis and Mary Pierce of France. American **Andre Agassi** captures the Men's title with a 3-6, 6-3, 6-2, 6-4 victory over the defending champion, Yevgeny Kafelnikov of Russia.

---

30 (Sunday): The St. Louis Rams win **Super Bowl XXXIV** at the Georgia Dome in Atlanta, with a 23-16 victory over the Tennessee Titans. With just over 2 minutes remaining and the score tied at 16, Kurt Warner connects with Isaac Bruce for a game-breaking 73-yard TD. On the last play of the game, Titans wide receiver Kevin Dyson is tackled on the St. Louis one-yard line by linebacker Mike Jones to preserve the win.

31 (Monday): **Chart Toppers:** The #1 song on the Billboard Hot 100 Singles Music Chart is "I Knew I Loved You" by Savage Garden.

Comic book artist of such memorable characters as "The Green Lantern", "Atom", "Spider Man", "The Hulk" and "Captain Marvel", **Gil Kane**, 73, dies of cancer in Miami, Florida.

(Tuesday): Titans WR Kevin Dyson is tackled on the 1-yard line by Mike Jones of the Rams. (See January 30th)

(Thursday): "CSNY2K" For the first time in 25 years Crosby, Stills, Nash, and Young perform on tour together. (See January 24th)

TIME · PASSAGES

FEBRUARY *2000*

Veteran Carlos Santana and newcomer Christina Aguilera at the Grammy Awards.

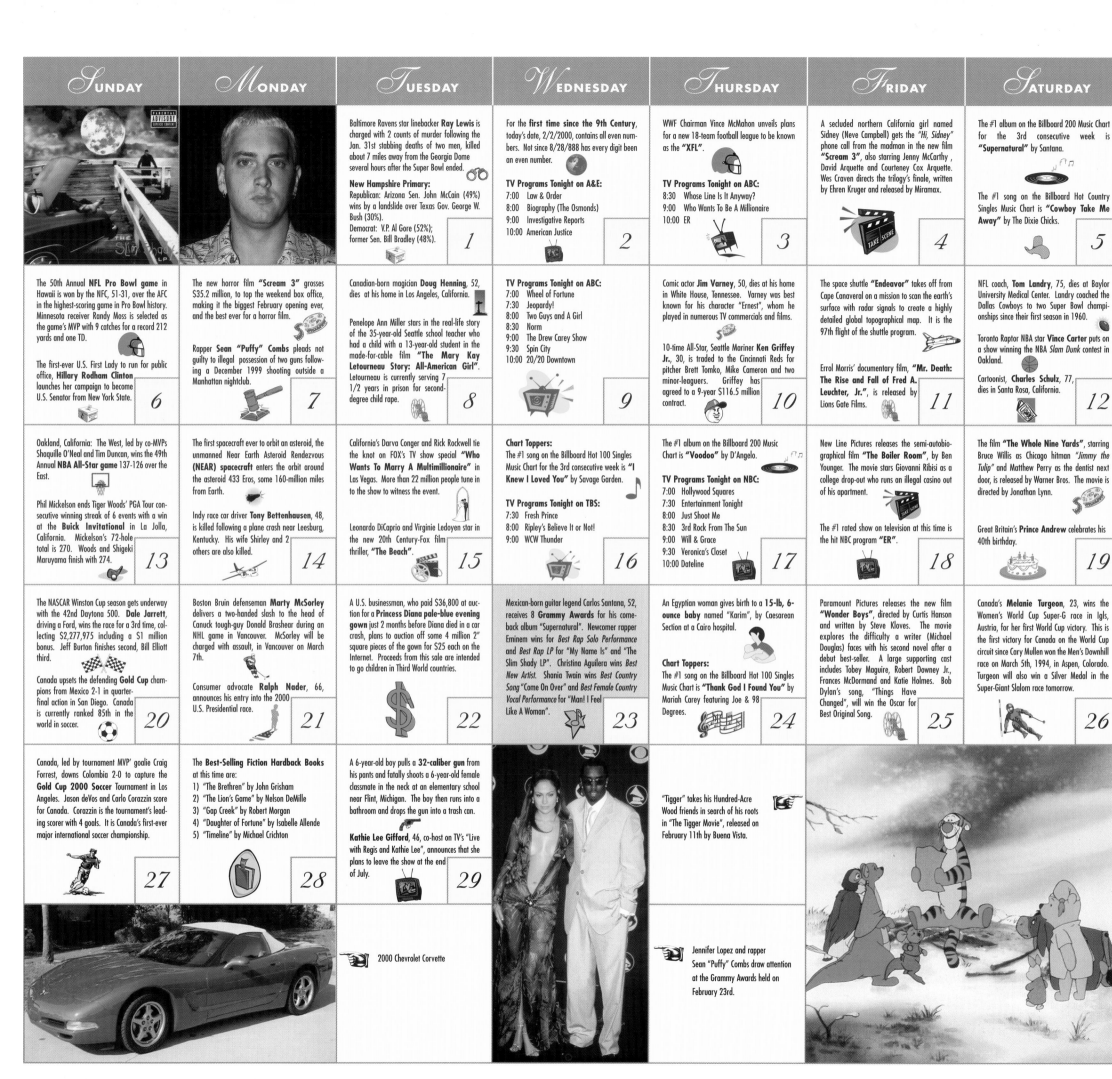

Sunday	Monday	Tuesday	Wednesday	Thursday	Friday	Saturday

Tuesday 1 — Baltimore Ravens star linebacker **Ray Lewis** is charged with 2 counts of murder following the Jan. 31st stabbing deaths of two men, killed about 7 miles away from the Georgia Dome several hours after the Super Bowl ended.

New Hampshire Primary:
Republican: Arizona Sen. John McCain (49%) wins by a landslide over Texas Gov. George W. Bush (30%).
Democrat: V.P. Al Gore (52%); former Sen. Bill Bradley (48%).

Wednesday 2 — For the **first time since the 9th Century**, today's date, 2/2/2000, contains all even numbers. Not since 8/28/888 has every digit been an even number.

TV Programs Tonight on A&E:
7:00 Law & Order
8:00 Biography (The Osmonds)
9:00 Investigative Reports
10:00 American Justice

Thursday 3 — WWF Chairman Vince McMahon unveils plans for a new 18-team football league to be known as the "**XFL**".

TV Programs Tonight on ABC:
8:30 Whose Line Is It Anyway?
9:00 Who Wants To Be A Millionaire
10:00 ER

Friday 4 — A secluded northern California girl named Sidney (Neve Campbell) gets the "Hi, Sidney" phone call from the madman in the new film "**Scream 3**", also starring Jenny McCarthy, David Arquette and Courteney Cox Arquette. Wes Craven directs the trilogy's finale, written by Ehren Kruger and released by Miramax.

Saturday 5 — The #1 album on the Billboard 200 Music Chart for the 3rd consecutive week is "**Supernatural**" by Santana.

The #1 song on the Billboard Hot Country Singles Music Chart is "**Cowboy Take Me Away**" by The Dixie Chicks.

Sunday 6 — The 50th Annual **NFL Pro Bowl game** in Hawaii is won by the NFC, 51-31, over the AFC in the highest-scoring game in Pro Bowl history. Minnesota receiver Randy Moss is selected as the game's MVP with 9 catches for a record 212 yards and one TD.

The first-ever U.S. First Lady to run for public office, **Hillary Rodham Clinton** launches her campaign to become U.S. Senator from New York State.

Monday 7 — The new horror film "**Scream 3**" grosses $35.2 million, to top the weekend box office, making it the biggest February opening ever, and the best ever for a horror film.

Rapper **Sean "Puffy" Combs** pleads not guilty to illegal possession of two guns following a December 1999 shooting outside a Manhattan nightclub.

Tuesday 8 — Canadian-born magician **Doug Henning**, 52, dies at his home in Los Angeles, California.

Penelope Ann Miller stars in the real-life story of the 35-year-old Seattle school teacher who had a child with a 13-year-old student in the made-for-cable film "**The Mary Kay Letourneau Story: All-American Girl**". Letourneau is currently serving 7 1/2 years in prison for second-degree child rape.

Wednesday 9 — **TV Programs Tonight on ABC:**
7:00 Wheel of Fortune
7:30 Jeopardy!
8:00 Two Guys and A Girl
8:30 Norm
9:00 The Drew Carey Show
9:30 Spin City
10:00 20/20 Downtown

Thursday 10 — Comic actor **Jim Varney**, 50, dies at his home in White House, Tennessee. Varney was best known for his character "Ernest", whom he played in numerous TV commercials and films.

10-time All-Star, Seattle Mariner **Ken Griffey Jr.**, 30, is traded to the Cincinnati Reds for pitcher Brett Tomko, Mike Cameron and two minor-leaguers. Griffey has agreed to a 9-year $116.5 million contract.

Friday 11 — The space shuttle "**Endeavor**" takes off from Cape Canaveral on a mission to scan the earth's surface with radar signals to create a highly detailed global topographical map. It is the 97th flight of the shuttle program.

Errol Morris' documentary film, "**Mr. Death: The Rise and Fall of Fred A. Leuchter, Jr.**", is released by Lions Gate Films.

Saturday 12 — NFL coach, **Tom Landry**, 75, dies at Baylor University Medical Center. Landry coached the Dallas Cowboys to two Super Bowl championships since their first season in 1960.

Toronto Raptor NBA star **Vince Carter** puts on a show winning the NBA *Slam Dunk* contest in Oakland.

Cartoonist, **Charles Schulz**, 77, dies in Santa Rosa, California.

Sunday 13 — Oakland, California: The West, led by co-MVPs Shaquille O'Neal and Tim Duncan, wins the 49th Annual **NBA All-Star game** 137-126 over the East.

Phil Mickelson ends Tiger Woods' PGA Tour consecutive winning streak of 6 events with a win at the **Buick Invitational** in La Jolla, California. Mickelson's 72-hole total is 270. Woods and Shigeki Maruyama finish with 274.

Monday 14 — The first spacecraft ever to orbit an asteroid, the unmanned **Near Earth Asteroid Rendezvous (NEAR) spacecraft** enters the orbit around the asteroid 433 Eros, some 160-million miles from Earth.

Indy race car driver **Tony Bettenhausen**, 48, is killed following a plane crash near Leesburg, Kentucky. His wife Shirley and 2 others are also killed.

Tuesday 15 — California's Darva Conger and Rick Rockwell tie the knot on FOX's TV show special "**Who Wants To Marry A Multimillionaire**" in Las Vegas. More than 22 million people tune in to the show to witness the event.

Leonardo DiCaprio and Virginie Ledoyen star in the new 20th Century-Fox film thriller, "**The Beach**".

Wednesday 16 — **Chart Toppers:**
The #1 song on the Billboard Hot 100 Singles Music Chart for the 3rd consecutive week is "**I Knew I Loved You**" by Savage Garden.

TV Programs Tonight on TBS:
7:30 Fresh Prince
8:00 Ripley's Believe It or Not!
9:00 WCW Thunder

Thursday 17 — The #1 album on the Billboard 200 Music Chart is "**Voodoo**" by D'Angelo.

TV Programs Tonight on NBC:
7:00 Hollywood Squares
7:30 Entertainment Tonight
8:00 Just Shoot Me
8:30 3rd Rock From The Sun
9:00 Will & Grace
9:30 Veronica's Closet
10:00 Dateline

Friday 18 — New Line Pictures releases the semi-autobiographical film "**The Boiler Room**", by Ben Younger. The movie stars Giovanni Ribisi as a college drop-out who runs an illegal casino out of his apartment.

The #1 rated show on television at this time is the hit NBC program "**ER**".

Saturday 19 — The film "**The Whole Nine Yards**", starring Bruce Willis as Chicago hitman *Jimmy the Tulip* and Matthew Perry as the dentist next door, is released by Warner Bros. The movie is directed by Jonathan Lynn.

Great Britain's **Prince Andrew** celebrates his 40th birthday.

Sunday 20 — The NASCAR Winston Cup season gets underway with the 42nd Daytona 500. **Dale Jarrett**, driving a Ford, wins the race for a 3rd time, collecting $2,277,975 including a $1 million bonus. Jeff Burton finishes second, Bill Elliott third.

Canada upsets the defending **Gold Cup** champions from Mexico 2-1 in quarter-final action in San Diego. Canada is currently ranked 85th in the world in soccer.

Monday 21 — Boston Bruin defenseman **Marty McSorley** delivers a two-handed slash to the head of Canuck tough-guy Donald Brashear during an NHL game in Vancouver. McSorley will be charged with assault, in Vancouver on March 7th.

Consumer advocate **Ralph Nader**, 66, announces his entry into the 2000 U.S. Presidential race.

Tuesday 22 — A U.S. businessman, who paid $36,800 at auction for a **Princess Diana pale-blue evening gown** just 2 months before Diana died in a car crash, plans to auction off some 4 million 2" square pieces of the gown for $25 each on the Internet. Proceeds from this sale are intended to go children in Third World countries.

Wednesday 23 — Mexican-born guitar legend Carlos Santana, 52, receives 8 **Grammy Awards** for his comeback album "Supernatural". Newcomer rapper Eminem wins for *Best Rap Solo Performance* and *Best Rap LP* for "My Name Is" and "The Slim Shady LP". Christina Aguilera wins *Best New Artist*. Shania Twain wins *Best Country Song* "Come On Over" and *Best Female Country Vocal Performance* for "Man! I Feel Like A Woman".

Thursday 24 — An Egyptian woman gives birth to a **15-lb, 6-ounce baby** named "Karim", by Caesarean Section at a Cairo hospital.

Chart Toppers:
The #1 song on the Billboard Hot 100 Singles Music Chart is "**Thank God I Found You**" by Mariah Carey featuring Joe & 98 Degrees.

Friday 25 — Paramount Pictures releases the new film "**Wonder Boys**", directed by Curtis Hanson and written by Steve Kloves. The movie explores the difficulty a writer (Michael Douglas) faces with his second novel after a debut best-seller. A large supporting cast includes Tobey Maguire, Robert Downey Jr., Frances McDormand and Katie Holmes. Bob Dylan's song, "Things Have Changed", will win the Oscar for Best Original Song.

Saturday 26 — Canada's **Melanie Turgeon**, 23, wins the Women's World Cup Super-G race in Igls, Austria, for her first World Cup victory. This is the first victory for Canada on the World Cup circuit since Cary Mullen won the Men's Downhill race on March 5th, 1994, in Aspen, Colorado. Turgeon will also win a Silver Medal in the Super-Giant Slalom race tomorrow.

Sunday 27 — Canada, led by tournament MVP' goalie Craig Forrest, downs Colombia 2-0 to capture the **Gold Cup 2000 Soccer** Tournament in Los Angeles. Jason deVos and Carlo Corazzin score for Canada. Corazzin is the tournament's leading scorer with 4 goals. It is Canada's first-ever major international soccer championship.

Monday 28 — The **Best-Selling Fiction Hardback Books** at this time are:
1) "The Brethren" by John Grisham
2) "The Lion's Game" by Nelson DeMille
3) "Gap Creek" by Robert Morgan
4) "Daughter of Fortune" by Isabelle Allende
5) "Timeline" by Michael Crichton

Tuesday 29 — A 6-year-old boy pulls a **32-caliber gun** from his pants and fatally shoots a 6-year-old female classmate in the neck at an elementary school near Flint, Michigan. The boy then runs into a bathroom and drops the gun into a trash can.

Kathie Lee Gifford, 46, co-host on TV's "Live with Regis and Kathie Lee", announces that she plans to leave the show at the end of July.

2000 Chevrolet Corvette

"Tigger" takes his Hundred-Acre Wood friends in search of his roots in "The Tigger Movie", released on February 11th by Buena Vista.

Jennifer Lopez and rapper Sean "Puffy" Combs draw attention at the Grammy Awards held on February 23rd.

Albert Finney and Julia Roberts star in the new film "Erin Brockovich".

Sunday	Monday	Tuesday	Wednesday	Thursday	Friday	Saturday

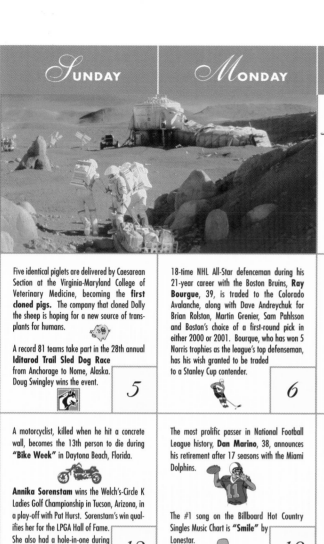

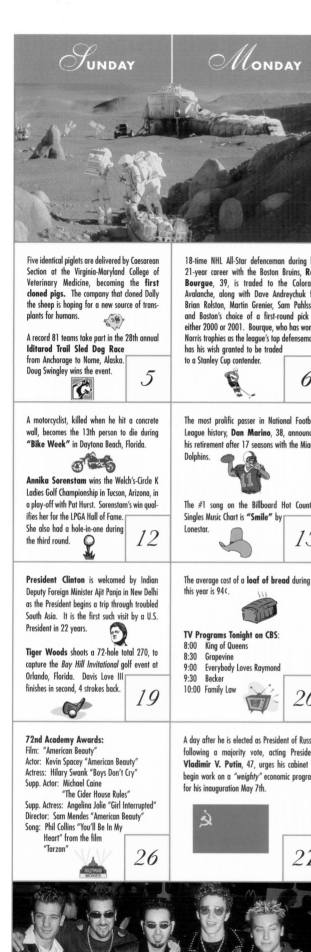

Tuesday (no date)
 The rescue crew reaches Mars in the new film "Mission to Mars". (See March 10th)

Wednesday 1
A study released in this month's issue of the journal **"Sexual Addiction and Compulsivity"** reports that at least 200,000 Internet users are hooked on porn sites, X-rated chat rooms or other sexual materials which are now available online.

Thursday 2
New Zealand becomes the first country, other than the U.S., to defend the 149-year-old **Americas Cup**, sweeping Italy 5-0 in the best-of-nine series off the coast of Auckland, New Zealand. Rookie skipper, Dean Barker, 26, was at the helm of "Black Magic". Veteran skipper Russell Coutts stepped aside before race 5 in favor of his protégé.

Friday 3
The star of the film "Free Willy", **Keiko, the killer whale**, leaves its enclosed pen in an Icelandic bay for a new area which is 22 times bigger. The *halfway house* in the bay is the first step in a possible release into the sea later this year. It is the first attempt to reintroduce a killer whale to the wild. Keiko was captured off Iceland more than 20 years ago when he was about two years old.

Saturday 4
Singers Whitney Houston and the artist formerly known as Prince receive **"Artist of the Decade"** awards at the annual *Soul Train Music Awards* in Los Angeles, California.

Only child "Willie" (Frankie Muniz) gets a puppy for his 9th birthday, in the film, **"My Dog Skip"**, co-starring Kevin Bacon and Diane Lane as his parents. The movie is directed by Jay Russell and is released by Warner Bros.

Sunday 5
Five identical piglets are delivered by Caesarean Section at the Virginia-Maryland College of Veterinary Medicine, becoming the **first cloned pigs**. The company that cloned Dolly the sheep is hoping for a new source of transplants for humans.

A record 81 teams take part in the 28th annual **Iditarod Trail Sled Dog Race** from Anchorage to Nome, Alaska. Doug Swingley wins the event.

Monday 6
18-time NHL All-Star defenceman during his 21-year career with the Boston Bruins, **Ray Bourque**, 39, is traded to the Colorado Avalanche, along with Dave Andreychuk for Brian Rolston, Martin Grenier, Sam Pahlsson and Boston's choice of a first-round pick in either 2000 or 2001. Bourque, who has won 5 Norris trophies as the league's top defenseman, has his wish granted to be traded to a Stanley Cup contender.

Tuesday 7
V.P. Al Gore sweeps all of the Democratic Presidential primaries on **Super Tuesday**. Gov. George W. Bush wins 9 of 13 Republican contests.

"Who Wants To Marry A Multimillionaire" bride, **Darva Conger**, 34, files for an annulment from TV husband Rick Rockwell, 42, claiming the marriage was never consummated.

Wednesday 8
Chart Toppers:
The #1 song on the Billboard Hot 100 Singles Music Chart is **"Amazed"** by Lonestar.

The #1 song on the Billboard Hot Country Singles Music Chart for the 2nd consecutive week is **"My Best Friend"** by Tim McGraw.

Thursday 9
Mattel Inc. releases a new **Timeless Treasures** celebrity doll, featuring Elizabeth Taylor as "Cleopatra" from the 1963 film. Taylor's first authorized portrait doll sells for $75.

A revival of Sam Shepard's 1980 play, **"True West"**, opens at the Circle in the Square, in New York City.

Friday 10
Buena Vista Pictures releases the new Brian DePalma sci-fi adventure film, **"Mission to Mars"**, starring Gary Sinise, Don Cheadle and Tim Robbins.

Pope John Paul II approves the canonization of Philadelphia, Pennsylvania nun **Katharine Drexel**. She will become the second U.S. born Saint on October 1st.

Saturday 11
The Formula One racing season gets under way in Melbourne, Australia. Ferrari's **Michael Schumacher** wins the race with teammate Rubens Barrichello second.

Toronto Maple Leaf defenceman **Brian Berard** suffers a career-ending eye injury when he is struck by the stick of Ottawa Senator Marian Hossa. He will have his retina re-attached in a 4 1/2-hour operation on March 21st.

Sunday 12
A motorcyclist, killed when he hit a concrete wall, becomes the 13th person to die during **"Bike Week"** in Daytona Beach, Florida.

Annika Sorenstam wins the Welch's-Circle K Ladies Golf Championship in Tucson, Arizona, in a play-off with Pat Hurst. Sorenstam's win qualifies her for the LPGA Hall of Fame. She also had a hole-in-one during the third round.

Monday 13
The most prolific passer in National Football League history, **Dan Marino**, 38, announces his retirement after 17 seasons with the Miami Dolphins.

The #1 song on the Billboard Hot Country Singles Music Chart is **"Smile"** by Lonestar.

Tuesday 14
Republican George W. Bush and Democrat Al Gore clinch their **Presidential nominations** in a series of southern state primaries.

Stephen King's new 66-page ghost story, "Riding the Bullet", is distributed exclusively on the Internet, available on e-book for downloading @ $2.50 U.S. It will receive over 400,000 orders during the first 24-hours.

Wednesday 15
Durwood Kirby, 88, dies of congestive heart failure at a nursing home in Fort Myers, Florida. The versatile TV funnyman played the second banana on "The Garry Moore Show" (1950's & 1960's) and also co-hosted his hit television series "Candid Camera" from 1961-66.

Thursday 16
A crazed man breaks into the locked cockpit of an **Alaska Airlines jet** en route to San Francisco, and grabs the controls. He is wrestled to the ground by terrified passengers as the pilot pleads for help over the intercom.

Johnny Depp stars as a sleazy New York City rare book dealer in the film **"The Ninth Gate"**. Released by Artisan, the movie also stars Frank Langella as an equally immoral business tycoon.

Friday 17
Julia Roberts stars as an unlikely law clerk who makes history taking on a major power company in a deadly water contamination cover-up, in the true-life film **"Erin Brockovich"**. Albert Finney co-stars as small-time lawyer "Ed Masry". The film is directed by Steven Soderbergh and released by Universal Pictures. Julia Roberts will win *Best Actress Oscar* for her performance.

Saturday 18
Chart Toppers:
The #1 song on the Billboard Hot 100 Singles Music Chart is **"Say My Name"** by Destiny's Child.

American **Neil Walker**, 23, sets a new world record in the Men's 100-metre Individual Medley final at the World Short Course Swimming Championships in Athens, Greece. It is his fourth world record at the meet.

Sunday 19
President Clinton is welcomed by Indian Deputy Foreign Minister Ajit Panja in New Delhi as the President begins a trip through troubled South Asia. It is the first such visit by a U.S. President in 22 years.

Tiger Woods shoots a 72-hole total 270, to capture the *Bay Hill Invitational* golf event at Orlando, Florida. Davis Love III finishes in second, 4 strokes back.

Monday 20
The average cost of a **loaf of bread** during this year is 94¢.

TV Programs Tonight on CBS:
8:00 King of Queens
8:30 Grapevine
9:00 Everybody Loves Raymond
9:30 Becker
10:00 Family Law

Tuesday 21
79-year-old **Pope John Paul II** continues his long desired visit to the Middle East and the sacred sites associated with the beginnings of Christianity. The Pope began his tour of Holy Land sites late in February. Today the Pope visits Israel expressing deep sorrow over the long suffering of the Jewish people.

Wednesday 22
The #1 album on the Billboard 200 Music Chart for the 4th consecutive week is **"Supernatural"** by Santana.

The price of **unleaded gasoline** now averages $1.38 per gallon.

Thursday 23
The Broadway musical, **"Aida"**, opens at the Palace Theater in N.Y.C., starring Heather Headley, Sherie Rene Scott and Adam Pascal. The musical will win four Tony Awards, including the *Best Actress* honor for Headley and *Best Original Score* for Elton John & Tim Rice.

Friday 24
TV Shows Tonight on NBC:
7:00 Hollywood Squares
7:30 Entertainment Tonight
8:00 Providence
9:00 Dateline
10:00 Law& Order Special Victims

Saturday 25
The #1 song on the Billboard Hot Country Singles Music Chart for the 2nd consecutive week is **"How Do You Like Me Now?"** by Toby Keith.

TV Shows Tonight On FOX:
7:30 Simpsons
8:00 COPS
8:30 COPS
9:00 America's Most Wanted
10:00 America's Dumbest Criminals

Sunday 26
72nd Academy Awards:
Film: "American Beauty"
Actor: Kevin Spacey "American Beauty"
Actress: Hilary Swank "Boys Don't Cry"
Supp. Actor: Michael Caine "The Cider House Rules"
Supp. Actress: Angelina Jolie "Girl Interrupted"
Director: Sam Mendes "American Beauty"
Song: Phil Collins "You'll Be In My Heart" from the film "Tarzan"

Monday 27
A day after he is elected as President of Russia following a majority vote, acting President **Vladimir V. Putin**, 47, urges his cabinet to begin work on a *"weighty"* economic program for his inauguration May 7th.

Tuesday 28
The new album **"No Strings Attached"** by 'N Sync sells a record 2.4 million copies in the United States during its first week of release. The band's second album broke the previous record of 1.1 million first-week sales by The Back Street Boys' "Millennium", which was released during May of 1999.

Wednesday 29
The 2000 **Major League Baseball** season opens in Japan at the Tokyo Dome as the Chicago Cubs down the NY Mets 5-3. The Cubs' 3rd baseman, Shane Andrews, hits the first home run of the 21st Century. Jon Lieber records the win and Mike Hampton the loss. 55,000 watch the earliest MLB season opener. Fans in New York and Chicago get to watch the game on TV, starting at 5:06am EST.

Thursday 30
Aleksei Yagudin of Russia captures his third straight Men's World Figure Skating title, winning the Gold Medal in Nice, France. Elvis Stojko of Canada wins Silver and American Michael Weiss wins the Bronze.

The Houston Astros open their new park, **Enron Field**, with an exhibition game against the New York Yankees.

Friday 31
DreamWorks releases the new animated film **"The Road to El Dorado"**, starring "Tulio" (Kevin Kline) and "Miguel" (Kenneth Branagh) as a wise-cracking duo in search of gold. The voice of "Chel" is provided by Rosie Perez. The music is supplied by Elton John and Tim Rice.

Universal Pictures releases **"The Skulls"**, starring Joshua Jackson and Paul Walker. Rob Cohen directs the film about a powerful secret society.

 'N Sync and their record-selling new LP "No Strings Attached". (See March 28th)

 Julia Roberts plays the real-life law clerk in the new film "Erin Brockovich". (See March 17th)

Frankie Muniz in a scene from the new film "My Dog Skip". (See March 4th)

Elian Gonzalez is taken by force from the home of his relatives in Little Havana, Miami.

Sunday	Monday	Tuesday	Wednesday	Thursday	Friday	Saturday

"Copenhagen" director Michael Blakemore displays his two Tony Awards. (See April 11th & June 4th)

Women's World Figure Skating Champion Michelle Kwan. (See April 1st)

Destiny's Child has the #1 single "Say My Name". (See April 4th)

1 — **Michelle Kwan** of the U.S. captures her third Women's World Figure Skating title in Nice, France. Russia's Irina Slutskaya and Maria Butyrskaya win the Silver and Bronze Medals respectively.

The #1 song on the Billboard Hot Country Singles Music Chart for the 3rd consecutive week is **"How Do You Like Me Now?"** by Toby Keith.

2 — Connecticut wins the **Women's NCAA Basketball** title, 71-52, over Tennessee in Philadelphia, Pa. The Connecticut Huskies are led by guard Shea Ralph, who scores 15 points and records 6 steals, to be named the MVP of the *Final Four*. Forward Svetlana Abrosimova scores 14 points and center Kelly Schumacher blocks an NCAA championship game record nine shots. Tennessee forward Tamika Catchings scores a game-high 16 points.

3 — A U.S. Federal judge rules that **Microsoft Corp.** violated antitrust laws as Microsoft shares fall $15.37 to close at $90.87. As a result of the decision, the NASDAQ composite index will record its largest single-day point swing tomorrow.

Michigan State wins the NCAA Men's Basketball Tournament in Indianapolis, Ind., 89-76, over Florida. Mateen Cleaves is named as the Final Four MVP.

4 — **Chart Toppers:**
The top 5 songs on the Billboard Hot 100 Singles Music Chart are:
1) "Say My Name", Destiny's Child
2) "Maria Maria", Santana featuring the Product G&B
3) "Breathe", Faith Hill
4) "Amazed", Lonestar
5) "Bye Bye Bye", 'N Sync

5 — The comic play **"The Graduate"** opens at the Gielgud Theatre in London, England, starring Kathleen Turner and Matthew Rhys. The screenplay written by Calder Willingham and Buck Henry is based on the hit 1967 film.

Patriarch of one of stock car racing's royal families, **Lee Petty** 86, dies in Greensboro, North Carolina. The father of Winston Cup great, Richard Petty, Lee won the first *Daytona 500* in 1959.

6 — The father of **Elian Gonzalez** arrives in the U.S., with his new wife and infant son, in hopes of being reunited with his son. They have been apart for 137 days since Elian fled Cuba with his mother.

7 — MGM releases the new romantic comedy film **"Return To Me"** starring David Duchovny and Minnie Driver. Bonnie Hunt co-stars, co-writes (with Canadian Don Lake) and directs the film.

8 — The University of North Dakota wins the **NCCA Division 1 Hockey Championship** with a 4-2 win over Boston College in Providence, Rhode Island. North Dakota's Lee Goren is named as the *Most Outstanding Player of the Froze Four*. Boston captain Mike Mottau was named as the winner of the Hobey Baker Memorial Award on April 7th.

9 — **Vijay Singh** of Fiji shoots a 10-under-par 278 to win the 64th Masters golf tournament at the Augusta (Ga.) National Golf Club. Ernie Els finishes in second, 3 strokes back.

The **Canadian Women's Hockey Team** wins its 6th straight world title with a 3-2 overtime victory over the U.S., at Mississauga's Hershey Centre in Ontario, Canada.

10 — **James McDermott Jr.**, 48, former top Wall Street executive, goes on trial in N.Y.C. for allegedly sharing inside stock information with his porn star mistress, Canadian Kathryn Gannon. He will be found guilty April 27th.

Cincinnati outfielder **Ken Griffey Jr.** (30 years, 141 days) becomes the youngest major leaguer to hit 400 career home runs. He surpasses Jimmie Foxx who was 30 years, 248 days old when he set the mark.

11 — The dramatic play **"Copenhagen"** opens on Broadway at the Royale Theater, starring Michael Cumpsty, Philip Bosco and Blair Brown, who will win the Tony for *Best Featured Actress* in a Play. Michael Blakemore will win the Tony for *Best Director* of the Tony award-winning play.

BROADWAY

Detroit's new $300-million **Comerica Park** opens with the Tigers winning 5-2 over Seattle, while the San Francisco Giants open their new park, **Pacific Bell**, against the LA Dodgers.

12 — Academy Award-winning actor, **Anthony Hopkins**, 62, renounces his British citizenship to become a U.S. citizen. Hopkins, who was knighted by Queen Elizabeth II in 1993, was required to recite the words *"I further renounce the title of nobility to which I have herefore belonged"*.

13 — Little Havana, Miami: A large group of anti-Castro Hispanics gather outside the house where **Elian Gonzalez** is being kept. The boy's great uncle defies the U.S. government's demand to hand him over to his father for return to Cuba. Cuban Americans singer Gloria Estefan and actor Andy Garcia, join in the demonstration.

The jazz musical **"The Wild Party"** opens at the Virginia Theater in New York City.

BROADWAY

14 — 100,000 Serbs rally in the main square of the Yugoslav capital of **Belgrade**, calling for the opposition leaders to appeal to President Slobodan Milosevic for an early election.

Lions Gate Films releases the savage satire **"American Psycho"** starring Chloe Sevigny and Christian Bale as the "yuppie killer".

15 — **NHL Season Leaders:**
Points: Jaromir Jagr (Pittsburgh) 96
Goals: Pavel Bure (Florida) 58
Assists: Mark Recchi (Philadelphia) 63
Penalty Minutes: Denny Lambert (Atlanta) 219
Goals-Against Average: Brian Boucher (Philadelphia) 1.91
The St. Louis Blues finish with the best overall record, with 51 wins, 20 losses, 11 ties, 1 RT for 114 pts.

16 — Canadian **Paul Tracy** wins the CART Grand Prix Auto Race in Long Beach, California. Helio Castro-Neves comes in second with Jimmy Vasser third.

The Cleveland Browns select Penn State defensive lineman Courtney Brown with the first overall pick, at the **NFL draft** of college players at Madison Square Garden in New York City. 1999 Heisman Trophy winner Ron Dayne is selected 11th by the NY Giants.

17 — In the closest finish in the race's 104-year history, Elijah Legat, 33, of Kenya, wins the **Boston Marathon** by a stride over Ethiopia's Gezahenge Abera. Catherine Ndereba, 27, is the top female finisher. Kenya's men have now won a record 10 consecutive Boston Marathons.

"The Real Thing" by Tom Stoppard opens at the Ethel Barrymore Theater in N.Y.C., starring Stephen Dillane and Jennifer Ehle.

BROADWAY

18 — **Chart Toppers:**
The #1 song on the Billboard Hot 100 Singles Music Chart for the 2nd consecutive week is **"Maria Maria"** by Santana featuring The Product G&B.

The #1 album on the Billboard 200 Music Chart for the 2nd consecutive week is **"No Strings Attached"** by 'N Sync.

19 — Billed as the world's first virtual newscaster, **"Ananova"**, a green-haired big-eyed beauty with a slight American accent, makes her debut on the Internet in London, England, giving breaking-news bulletins.

President Clinton dedicates the **Oklahoma City National Memorial** on the 5th anniversary of the bombing of the Alfred P. Murrah federal building.

20 — **NBA Season Leaders:**
Scoring: Shaquille O'Neal (LA Lakers) 29.7 average, 2,344 pts.
Assists: Jason Kidd (Phoenix) 10.1 average, 678 total
Rebounds: Dikembe Mutombo (Atlanta) 14.1average, 1,157 total

The LA Lakers finish with the best overall record of 67 wins, 15 losses, .817 pct.

21 — The musical comedy **"Blue"**, about a black Southern family in the funeral business, opens at the Arena Stage's Kreeger Theater in Washington, D.C. The play, written by Charles Randolph-Wright with music by Nona Hendryx, stars Phylicia Rashad, Michael Wiggins, Messeret Stroman, Randall Shepperd and Arnold McCuller.

22 — Tensions in Miami, Florida, heat up as federal agents, armed with automatic weapons, storm the house of **Elian Gonzalez's** relatives and take the boy by force. He is flown to Andrews Air Force Base where he is reacquainted with his father. Rioting by demonstrators on the streets of Little Havana ensue with more than 180 people arrested.

Theatrical producer **Alexander Cohen**, 79, dies in N.Y.C.

BROADWAY

23 — Matthew McConaughey and Harvey Keitel co-star in the submarine drama **"U-571"**. A U.S. sub sets out to capture an enigma decoder machine from a disabled German U-boat in the Universal Pictures film. The supporting cast includes Bill Paxton, Jon Bon Jovi, Jake Weber and T.C. Carson. Jon Johnson will win his first Academy Award Oscar for his *sound editing* on the film.

ADMIT ONE

24 — The **space shuttle "Atlantis"**, scheduled to lift off today, is the first of the four shuttles to undergo a comprehensive overhaul. The new cockpit has 11 color screens with attention grabbing imagery patterned after those used in a Boeing 777. The liquid crystal flat panel cockpit displays that mimic the 1960's and 1970's era gauges were designed by Honeywell Space Systems. The first flight for Atlantis since 1977 will occur on May 19th.

25 — Broadway's most successful producer with over 80 productions, **David Merrick**, 88, dies in London, England. Merrick's body will be flown to the U.S. for burial. Some of his Broadway hits include "Gypsy", "Hello Dolly", and "42nd Street".

BROADWAY

Actor **Al Pacino** celebrates his 60th birthday.

26 — The **Top 5 Albums** on the Billboard 200 Music Chart at this time are:
1) "No Strings Attached", 'N Sync
2) "Return of Saturn", No Doubt
3) "Supernatural", Santana
4) "Unleash the Dragon", Sisqo
5) "Unrestricted", Da Brat

27 — 16 members of the Detroit Tigers and Chicago White Sox are suspended for a total of 82 games in what is believed to be the **harshest penalty for a brawl** in Major League Baseball history. The brawl occurred during a game on Saturday, April 22nd, at Chicago's Comiskey Park.

28 — Canada Post launches the **world's first personalized vanity postage stamps**. A customer can now insert a printed label made from a photo into a gold-colored picture frame.

It costs 39¢ to **mail a 1st-class letter** in the United States.

US MAIL

29 — The #1 song on the Billboard Hot Country singles Music Chart for the 2nd consecutive week is **"The Best Day"** by George Strait.

WBC & IBF Heavyweight Boxing champion **Lennox Lewis** of Britain retains his titles with a second-round knockout of Michael Grant during their bout in N.Y.C. Lewis was recently stripped of his WBA title for fighting Grant before contender John Ruiz.

30 — The **NY Knicks** down the Toronto Raptors 87-80 to sweep the Raptors first National Basketball Association play-off series. The game, played in Toronto, is the first and only post-season NBA game ever to have been played in Canada.

Matthew McConaughey leads a U.S. submarine crew in the film "U-571". (See April 23rd)

2000 Chrysler PT Cruiser

M A Y   2000

Sixteen contestants will compete for $1 million on the new game show "Survivor".

(Photo credit CBS Photo Archive)

Sunday	Monday	Tuesday	Wednesday	Thursday	Friday	Saturday
	Time Passages Commemorative Yearbooks are published. Claiming that they were undercompensated by the residual payment system employed by advertisers, members of the **Screen Actors Guild** and the **American Federation of Television and Radio Artists** begin a joint strike against advertisers. Indy Winner Juan Montoya. (See May 28th) **1**	For the first time since 1845, the state of Arkansas executes a woman, as convicted murderer **Christina Riggs**, 28, is put to death by lethal injection. Riggs becomes only the fifth woman to be executed in the U.S. since capital punishment was reinstated in 1976. The premiere issue of **"O: The Oprah Magazine"** by Oprah Winfrey is on sale. The May/June issue is entitled "Live Your Best Life!". **2**	The **Best-Selling Fiction Hardback Books** at this time are: 1) "Before I Say Goodbye" by Mary Higgins Clark 2) "Back Roads" by Tawni O'Dell 3) "The Wedding" by Danielle Steel 4) "The Brethren" by John Grisham 5) "Beowulf" translated by Seamus Heaney **3**	A U.S. government begins burning to clear brush near **Los Alamos, New Mexico.** The fire will rage out of control and destroy 400 homes and force approximately 25,000 people to flee. The historic buildings where scientists assembled the first atomic bomb during WW II will also be consumed by the wildfire. An e-mail virus dubbed the **"I Love You"** virus infects millions of computers around the world. **4**	Five planets, including the Sun and the Moon, are in the **tightest alignment** in the sky since 1962. However, the alignment of Mercury, Venus, Mars, Jupiter, Saturn and the Moon are obscured by the Sun's glare. Oscar-winning actors **Billy Bob Thornton**, 44, and Angelina Jolie, 24, are married in Las Vegas. It is his 5th marriage and her 2nd. **5**	**"Fusaichi Pegasus"**, with jockey Kent Desormeaux aboard, wins the 126th **Kentucky Derby**, running the 1 1/4-mile distance in 2:01.12. "Aptitude" places second with "Impeachment" finishing in third. "Fusaichi Pegasus" becomes the first favorite to win the run for the roses in 21 years. **6**
Philadelphia Flyers' **Andy Delmore** becomes the first rookie defenseman to score 3 goals in a Stanley Cup play-off game as Philly wins 6-3 over Pittsburgh in Philadelphia. Delmore now has 5 goals in the series, including the overtime winner in game 4. Producer, actor, author and businessman, **Douglas Fairbanks Jr.**, dies at the age of 90. **7**	Russell Crowe stars as the Roman army general "Maximus", who becomes a hero in the ring of the Roman coliseum, in the film **"Gladiator"**. Directed by Ridley Scott, the film uses computer-generated re-creations to show the Rome skyline circa 40 AD. Co-stars include Joaquin Phoenix as "Commodus Caesar" and Oliver Reed. The film will win five Oscars, including *Best Picture*, *Costumes*, *Visual Effects* and *Best Actor* for Crowe. The film is released by DreamWorks. **8**	**Celestis Inc.** is now taking reservations to bury the cremated remains of about 200 people on the Moon as early as next year. The group, who launched the cremated remains of LSD guru Timothy Leary and "Star Trek" creator Gene Roddenberry more than 3 years ago, charges $12,500 each for its services. **9**	The #1 song on the Billboard Hot Country Singles Music Chart is **"Buy Me A Rose"** by Kenny Rogers with Alison Krauss & Billy Dean. **TV Programs Tonight on ABC:** 8:00 Who Wants To Be A Millionaire 9:00 Spin City 10:00 20/20 **10**	By a vote of 62-48, the South Carolina House of Representatives votes to remove the **Confederate battle flag** from atop the State Capitol where it has flown since 1962. As of July 1st, the flag will be placed next to a Confederate monument in front of the Capitol building. **11**	NASCAR driver **Adam Petty**, 19, dies following a crash during practice at New Hampshire's International Speedway in Loudon, N.H. Family patriarch Lee Petty (Adam's great-grandfather) died five weeks ago. The **Bank of Canada** stops issuing the $1,000 bill, saying it is the most-often used bill to launder money and to illicitly transport large sums of cash back and forth across Canadian borders. **12**	John Travolta plays a *Psychlo alien* in the L. Ron Hubbard sci-fi adventure film **"Battlefield Earth"**. Roger Christian directs the Warner Bros. release. The film will win seven Golden Raspberry Awards, including *Worst Film*, *Worst Actor*, and *Worst Director*. Kevin Spacey and Danny De Vito play lubricant salesmen in **"The Big Kahuna"**. John Swanbeck directs the film released by Lions Gate Films. **13**
Washington, D.C.: Thousands of women march in the nation's capitol on **Mother's Day** to demand tougher gun laws. The six-member cast of the top-rated comedy show **"Friends"** sign a 2-year contract renewal, giving each of the stars $750,000 per episode. **14**	Indiana University basketball coach **Bobby Knight**, 59, is suspended for 3 games next season and fined $30,000 for his *"pattern of inappropriate behavior"*. Knight will also have to adhere to a code of conduct under a *"zero-tolerance policy"*. **15**	A fight breaks out in the stands at **Wrigley Field** between fans and players. 16 LA Dodgers players and 3 coaches will be suspended on May 24th. This will be the first time in baseball history that there have been so many suspensions from one altercation. **16**	The series finale of **"Beverly Hills 90210"** airs on FOX-TV. The two-hour finale sees Donna & David tie the knot. Canadian **Ben Webster** reaches the summit of Mt. Everest, the world's highest peak. Pope John Paul II celebrates his 80th birthday. **17**	The **Most-Watched TV shows** in the U.S. at this time are: 1) "Who Wants To Be A Millionaire" (ABC) 2) "ER" (NBC) 3) "Frasier" (NBC) 4) "Spin City" (ABC) 5) "Friends" (NBC) **18**	In an effort to stop the new **International Space Station** from spiralling toward Earth, the space shuttle "Atlantis" is launched with a mission to replace dying Russian batteries on the station and to boost its orbit. N.Y.C. mayor **Rudolph Giuliani**, 55, abandons his U.S. Senate campaign against rival Hillary Rodham Clinton. **19**	"Red Bullet", with jockey Jerry Bailey aboard, wins the 125th **Preakness**, upsetting Kentucky Derby winner "Fusaichi Pegasus". "Impeachment" finishes third in the 1 3/16 mile race. "Red Bullet" is owned by Canadian Frank Stronach. The last **F.A. Cup** final, played at London's Wembley Stadium (due for demolition in Oct.) is won by Chelsea 1-0 over Aston Villa. **20**
The Palme d'Or (Golden Palm) award at the 53rd **Cannes Film Festival** is awarded to the Danish film "Dancer in the Dark", directed by Lars Von Trier. Star of the film is Icelandic singer Bjork, who wins the *Best Actress* award in her film debut. Americans John E. Richards and James Flamberg win the *Best Screenplay* award for "Nurse Betty". Actor **Sir Arthur John Gielgud**, 96, dies at his home near London. **21**	CNN reporter **Bernard Shaw** turns 60. The NRA executive board unanimously re-elects **Charlton Heston** to a 3rd one-year-term as president. An Iguanodon named "Aladar" (voiced by Bob Sweeney) is raised by a family of lemurs in the animated film **"Dinosaur"**, released by Buena Vista. **22**	**Record-breaking low temperatures** sweep across California and Arizona, hitting 47°F in Lake Havasu City and 43°F in Phoenix. Temperatures in California hit 38°F across the state. Amateur golfer **Woody Harford**, 36, sinks a 100-foot putt at a Central Park, N.Y.C. promotion to launch a new golf magazine "Maximum Golf" and wins $1 million. **23**	**Michael J. Fox** appears in his last show of "Spin City" during the season finale. A study published in the Journal of the American Medical Association suggests that men who don't drink coffee are 5 times more likely to develop **Parkinson's disease** than coffee drinkers who drink 4 1/2-5 1/2, 6-ounce cups a day. **24**	Tom Cruise stars as Special Agent Ethan Hunt in the film sequel **"Mission: Impossible 2"** directed by John Woo. Cruise teams up with Thandie Newton and Ving Rhames to go up against Dougray Scott as the villain. The movie is released by Paramount. The #1 song on the Billboard Hot Country Singles Music Chart is **"The Way You Love Me"** by Faith Hill. **25**	A second e-mail virus called **"Killer Resumé"** affects U.S. computers. Buena Vista releases the cowboy film spoof **"Shanghai Noon"**, starring martial arts expert Jackie Chan and directed by Tom Dey. Owen Wilson and Lucy Liu co-star in the action-packed comedy film. **26**	National Hockey League *Hall-of-Famer*, **Maurice "Rocket" Richard**, 78, dies following a lengthy illness in a Montreal hospital. Richard won 8 Stanley Cups with the Canadiens during his 18-year career. Elected to the Hall of Fame in 1961, he was the first player to score 50 goals in a season, and 500 goals in a career. **27**
Defending CART champion Juan Montoya, 24, wins the 84th **Indianapolis 500** in his first attempt. Montoya is the first rookie to win the race since Graham Hill performed the feat in 1966. Buddy Lazier finishes 7.183 seconds back in second place. Montoya collects $1,235,690. The two women in the race, Sarah Fisher, 19, and Lyn St. James, are forced out of the race when their cars make contact on lap 74. **28**	**Chart Toppers:** The #1 song on the Billboard Hot 100 Singles Music Chart for the 8th consecutive week is **"Maria Maria"** by Santana featuring the Product G&B. The #1 album on the Billboard 200 Music Chart for the 8th consecutive week is **"No Strings Attached"** by 'N Sync. **29**	The **New Jersey Devils** defeat their visiting Dallas Stars 7-3 in game one of the NHL Stanley Cup finals. The Devils' top line of Jason Arnott (2G, 2A), Peter Sykora (2G, 2A) and Patrik Elias (3A) lead the way for New Jersey. The **world's tallest skyscrapers**, the 452-meter-tall Petronas Twin Towers in Kuala Lumpur, Malaysia, opens to the public. **30**	CBS-TV premieres the new reality game show **"Survivor"**, hosted by Jeff Probst. Sixteen contestants are placed on a rat-infested island in the South China Sea, separated into two tribes, *Pagong* and *Tagi*. Each week tribe members compete for rewards and to see which tribe will have to vote off one of its members during the tribal council meeting at the end of each show. This week Sonja Christopher, 62, is the first to be voted off the island. **31**			
		Tom Cruise stars in the new film "Mission Impossible 2". (See May 25th)	Russell Crowe stars as the "Gladiator". (See May 8th)			

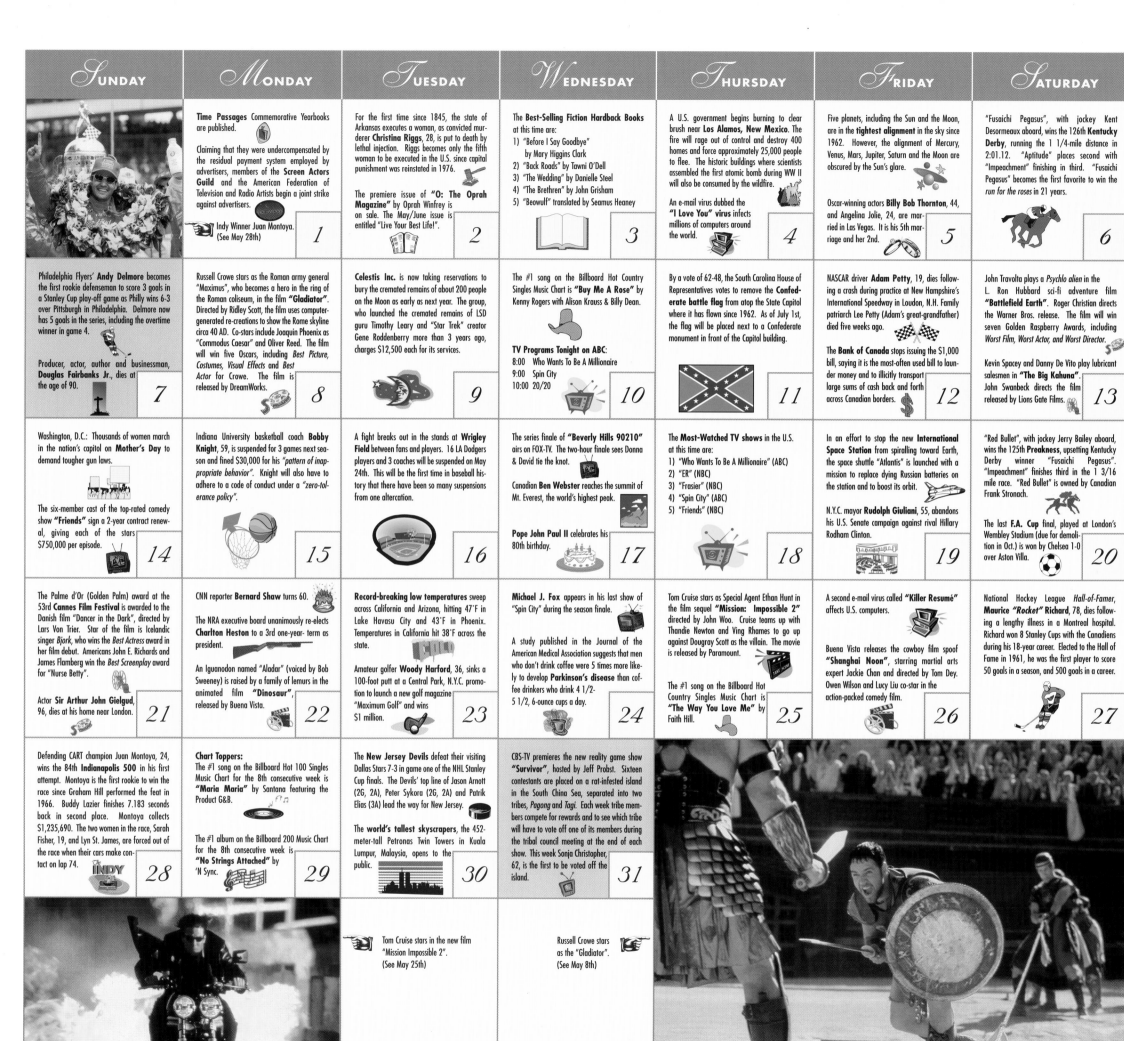

TIME·PASSAGES

JUNE 2000

L.A. Laker's Shaquille O'Neal hosts the NBA Championship Trophy and his MVP Award.

Sunday	Monday	Tuesday	Wednesday	Thursday	Friday	Saturday

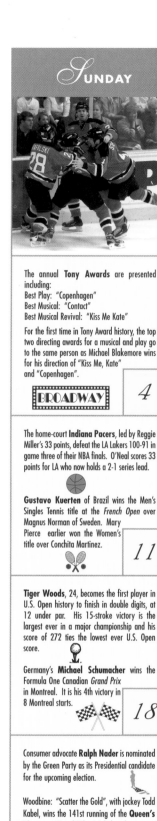

New Jersey Devil Jason Arnott (A) celebrates his Stanley Cup winning goal in game 6. (See June 10th)

Mel Gibson stars in the new film "The Patriot". (See June 29th)

1
Brett Hull scores 2 goals assisted by Mike Madano to lead the visiting Dallas Stars to a 2-1 victory over the New Jersey Devils. Dallas goalie Ed Belfour makes 27 saves allowing only Devil forward Alexander Mogilny to get one past him. The Stanley Cup finals are now tied at 1 game apiece.

2
New York City officials fail in their bid to stop photographer Spencer Tunick from **photographing 150 nudes** on a city street June 4th as part of this Naked States Tour.

The average cost of **unleaded gasoline** has risen to $1.49 per gallon.

3
The visiting **New Jersey Devils**, led by Jason Arnott with a goal and assist, defeat the Dallas Stars 2-1, at Reunion Arena to take a 2-1 Stanley Cup series lead. Petr Sykora scores the winner on a power play at 12:27 of the 2nd period.

The #1 album on the Billboard 200 Music Chart is **"Oops!....I Did It Again"** by Britney Spears.

4
The annual **Tony Awards** are presented including:
Best Play: "Copenhagen"
Best Musical: "Contact"
Best Musical Revival: "Kiss Me Kate"

For the first time in Tony Award history, the top two directing awards for a musical and play go to the same person as Michael Blakemore wins for his direction of "Kiss Me, Kate" and "Copenhagen".

BROADWAY

5
The visiting **NJ Devils** take a commanding 3-1 series lead in the Stanley Cup finals with a 3-1 victory over the Dallas Stars. Sergei Brylin, John Madden & Brian Rafalski score for New Jersey. Joe Nieuwendyk scores for Dallas.

Defending CART champion Juan Montoya, driving his Toyota, wins the **Miller Lite 225** at the Milwaukee Mile in West Allis, Wisconsin.

6
Chart Toppers:
The #1 song on the Billboard Hot 100 Singles Music Chart for the 9th consecutive week is **"Maria Maria"** by Santana featuring the Product G&B.

The #1 song on the Billboard Hot Country Singles Music Chart is **"The Way You Love Me"** by Faith Hill.

7
On the hit TV reality series **"Survivor"** B.B. is voted off the island.

The home-court **Los Angeles Lakers**, led by Shaquille O'Neal with a game-high 43 points and 19 rebounds, defeat the Indiana Pacers 104-87 in game one of the NBA championship series.

8
The **Dallas Stars** avoid elimination when Mike Madano beats NJ Devils goaltender Martin Brodeur at 6:21 of the third overtime period as the Stars defeat the visiting Devils 1-0 in game 5 of the Stanley Cup finals. In a great display of goaltending Ed Belfour makes 48 saves for Dallas while Martin Brodeur turns aside 40 for New Jersey.

9
The home-court **LA Lakers** take a 2-0 series lead with a 111-104 victory over the Indiana Pacers. Shaquille O'Neal scores 40 points with Glen Rice and Ron Harper adding 21 points each for the winners. O'Neal went to the foul line a record 39 times, missing 21 times. LA Lakers star Kobe Bryant left the game on crutches halfway through the first quarter.

10
Long-shot "Commendable", with jockey Pat Day aboard, wins the 132nd **Belmont Stakes**. "Aptitude" places second with "Unshaded" third.

The N.J. Devils win the Stanley Cup when Jason Arnott scores at 8:20 in the 2nd period of over-time to give the Devils a 2-1 victory over the Dallas Stars. Devils defenceman Scott Stevens wins the series Conn Smythe MVP trophy.

11
The home-court **Indiana Pacers**, led by Reggie Miller's 33 points, defeat the LA Lakers 100-91 in game three of their NBA finals. O'Neal scores 33 points for LA who now holds a 2-1 series lead.

Gustavo Kuerten of Brazil wins the Men's Singles Tennis title at the *French Open* over Magnus Norman of Sweden. Mary Pierce earlier won the Women's title over Conchita Martinez.

12
San Francisco quarterback **Steve Young**, 38, announces his retirement from football. Young leaves with the highest career pass rating in NFL history, 96.8.

Energy Department officials announce that highly sensitive information about **nuclear weapons**, contained on two computer hard drives, has gone missing from a vault at the Los Alamos National Laboratory in New Mexico.

13
The **American Film Institute's** list of the 100 funniest American movies is released including:
1) "Some Like It Hot" (1959)
2) "Tootsie" (1982)
3) "Dr. Strangelove, or: How I Learned to Stop Worrying and Love the Bomb" (1964)
4) "Annie Hall" (1977)
5) "Duck Soup" (1933)
6) "Blazing Saddles" (1974)
7) "M*A*S*H" (1970)
8) "It Happened One Night" (1934)

14
On the hit TV show **"Survivor"** Stacey is voted off the island.

The visiting **LA Lakers** take a commanding 3-1 series lead with a 120-118 overtime victory over the Indiana Pacers. Kobe Bryant, 21, who missed game 3 with a sprained ankle, scores 28 points, including 8 in overtime, to lead the Lakers to victory.

15
NHL Trophy Winners:
Art Ross (Scoring): Jaromir Jagr (Pittsburgh)
Hart (MVP): Chris Pronger (St. Louis)
Norris (Defense): Chris Pronger (St. Louis)
Vezina (Goal): Olaf Kolzig (Washington)
Calder (Rookie): Scott Gomez (New Jersey)
Lady Byng (Sportsmanship): Pavol Demitra (St. Louis)
Jack Adams (Coach): Joel Quenneville (St. Louis)

16
The home-court **Indiana Pacers** avoid elimination with a 120-87 thrashing of the LA Lakers. Jalen Rose scores 32 with Reggie Miller adding 25 for the Pacers. O'Neal scores a game-high 35 points in defeat.

20th Centruy-Fox releases the computer-generated sci-fi film **"Titan A.E."** with the voices of Matt Damon and Drew Barrymore.

17
"Sugar" Shane Mosley becomes the new WBC Welterweight champion in a 12-round split decision over defending champ Oscar De La Hoya in Los Angeles.

18
Tiger Woods, 24, becomes the first player in U.S. Open history to finish in double digits, at 12 under par. His 15-stroke victory is the largest ever in a major championship and his score of 272 ties the lowest ever U.S. Open score.

Germany's **Michael Schumacher** wins the Formula One Canadian *Grand Prix* in Montreal. It is his 4th victory in 8 Montreal starts.

19
The home-court **LA Lakers win the NBA championship** in game 6 with a 116-111 victory over the Indiana Pacers. Shaquille O'Neal, who scores a game-high 41 points, is selected to receive the series MVP award, becoming only the third player in league history to be named the season MVP, finals MVP and All-Star MVP in the same season. O'Neal averaged a series-high 38 points and 16.7 rebounds per game.

20
Hiawatha G. Knight of Detroit is believed to be the first woman to head one of boxing's major sanctioning organizations, as she is elected President of the International Boxing Federation (IBF).

The first permanent implant of an electric heart (the **Jarvik 2000**) takes place at the Oxford Heart Centre in England.

21
Britain's **Prince William** celebrates his 18th birthday.

On the TV show **"Survivor"** Ramona is voted off the island.

Two-time Hall-of-famer, **Lenny Wilkens** is introduced as the Toronto Raptors' new coach. Wilkens has won more games than any coach in NBA history.

22
Chart Toppers:
The #1 song on the Billboard Hot 100 Singles Music Chart is **"Try Again"** by Aaliyah.

NASA announces that images sent back to Earth from the **Mars Global Surveyor** contain evidence that there might be sources of liquid water on, or just below, the surface of the planet Mars.

23
20th Century-Fox releases the new Farrelly Brothers comedy film **"Me, Myself and Irene"** starring Renee Zellweger and Jim Carrey, who plays both a good cop and bad cop.

DreamWorks releases **"Chicken Run"**, the Claymation comedy cartoon version of the classic action film "The Great Escape". Circus rooster "Rocky" (voiced by Mel Gibson) shows the hens the way to freedom.

24
NHL Draft:
Boston University goalie Rick DiPietro is the first player selected overall at the annual NHL draft, by the NY Islanders.
2) Atlanta - LW Danny Heatley - Wisconsin U
3) Minn. LW Marian Gaborik - Dukla, Slovakia

Boxer **Mike Tyson** takes 38 seconds to knock-out Lou Savarese at Hampden Park in Glasgow, Scotland. Tyson earns $8 million.

25
Consumer advocate **Ralph Nader** is nominated by the Green Party as its Presidential candidate for the upcoming election.

Woodbine: "Scatter the Gold", with jockey Todd Kabel, wins the 141st running of the **Queen's Plate** over "I and I" by 4 1/2 lengths.

Juli Inkster wins the LPGA championship at Wilmington, Delaware, in a play-off with Stefania Croce.

26
Scientists announce that they have compiled a working draft of the **human genetic code**, ending a decade-long race that has cost billions of dollars. Scientists from the *Human Genome Project* and *Celera Genomics* completed the first draft of the human genetic code which will be used to detect and fight disease.

27
Chart Toppers:
The #1 song on the Billboard Hot 100 Singles Music Chart is **"Be With You"** by Enrique Iglesias.

For the **first time in four decades**, the U.S. House Republicans cut a deal to allow direct sale of food to Cuba.

28
Cincinnati's **Kenyon Martin** is selected first overall by the New Jersey Nets at the annual National Basketball Association draft.

In a 5-4 decision, the U.S. Supreme Court rules that the **Boy Scouts** may exclude gays from serving as Troop Leaders.

On the hit TV show **"Survivor"** Dirk is voted off the island.

29
The #1 album on the Billboard 200 Music Chart for the 3rd consecutive week is **"The Marshall Mathers LP"** by Eminem.

Mel Gibson stars as the "Swamp Fox' Francis Marian, who led a charge against the Redcoats during the American Revolution, in the film **"The Patriot"**. Co-stars include Heath Ledger as Gibson's oldest son, and Jason Isaacs. The film is directed by Roland Emmerich and is released by Sony.

30
Universal Pictures releases the a remake of the 1960's cartoon series, **"The Adventures of Rocky and Bullwinkle"**. René Russo and Jason Alexander star as villains "Natasha" & "Boris" with Robert De Niro as their fearless leader.

George Clooney, Mark Walberg and Diane Lane star in the epic drama **"The Perfect Storm"**, directed by Wolfgang Petersen and released by Warner Bros. Pictures.

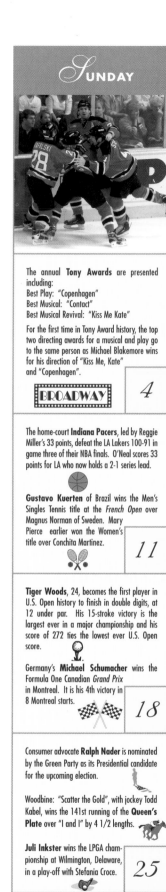

Jim Carrey and Renee Zellweger in a scene from the new film "Me, Myself & Irene". (See June 23rd)

Samuel L. Jackson stars as private eye "John Shaft" in the latest film based on the 1970's icon which originally starred Richard Roundtree. The film "Shaft" is released by Paramount on June 16th.

Mark Wahlberg and George Clooney meet the mother of all waves in the new film "The Perfect Storm". (See June 30th)

JULY

2000

Venus and Serena Williams capture the Women's Doubles Tennis Title at Wimbledon.

Sunday	Monday	Tuesday	Wednesday	Thursday	Friday	Saturday

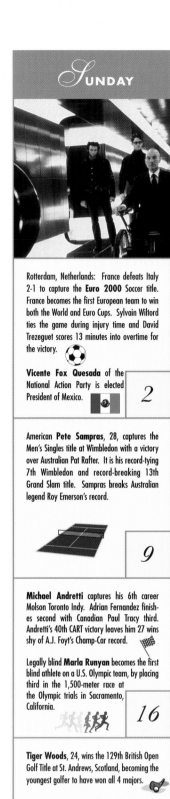

"Professor X" (Patrick Stewart) leads a group of good guy mutants in the new film The X-Men". (See July 17th)

Pete Sampras wins his 7th Men's Single's Tennis title at Wimbledon. (See July 9th)

Author J.K. Rowlings with her 4th book in the popular Harry Potter children's series. (See July 8th)

1

Capt. Cynthia Anderson becomes the first woman to stand guard at London's Buckingham Palace. She is part of a contingent of 150 Australians who are temporarily guarding the palace to mark *Australia Week*.

Oscar-winning actor, **Walter Matthau**, 79, dies of a heart attack in Santa Monica, California.

2

Rotterdam, Netherlands: France defeats Italy 2-1 to capture the **Euro 2000** Soccer title. France becomes the first European team to win both the World and Euro Cups. Sylvain Wiltord ties the game during injury time and David Trezeguet scores 13 minutes into overtime for the victory.

Vicente Fox Quesada of the National Action Party is elected President of Mexico.

3

The **Best-Selling Mass-Market Paperbacks** at this time are:
1) "The Perfect Storm" by Sebastian Junger
2) "Hannibal" by Thomas Harris
3) "Irish Hearts" by Nora Roberts
4) "Tom Clancy's Op Center: Divide and Conquer" by Tom Clancy and Steve Pieczenik
5) "Irish Rebel" by Nora Roberts

4

The U.S. retains the second annual match-play tournament **"Nation's Cup"** at the Emerald Hills Golf Club in Stouffville, Ontario, Canada. The two 5-women teams from Canada and the U.S. tie at 4 1/2 points, allowing the U.S. to retain the title.

NY Yankees owner **George Steinbrenner** turns 70.

5

The TV show **"Big Brother"** debuts on CBS-TV. 10 contestants enter their new home in California, with 28 cameras and 16 microphones. The winner will get $500,000 for surviving a 3-month stay.

On the TV show **"Survivor"**, Joel Klug is voted off the island.

Actor **Sean Connery** is knighted by Queen Elizabeth II.

6

The U.S. Postal Service unveils its new **"Legends of Baseball"** postage stamps that include images of former stars Jackie Robinson and Hank Aaron.

The #1 song on the Billboard Hot Country Singles Music Chart for the 3rd consecutive week is **"Yes!"** by Chad Brock.

7

NASCAR loses a second driver as **Kenny Irwin**, 30, is killed when he slams into the wall during practice at N.H. International Speedway.

The #1 album on the Billboard 200 Music Chart for the 5th consecutive week is **"The Marshall Mathers LP"** by Eminem.

Former Beatle **Ringo Starr** turns 60.

8

Venus Williams, 20, wins her first Grand Slam Tennis title with a straight sets victory over fellow-American Lindsay Davenport, at Wimbledon. Venus, along with sister Serena, 18, will become the first sisters to capture the women's Wimbledon Doubles championship on July 10th.

"Harry Potter and the Goblet of Fire" by J.K. Rowlings is now on sale in bookstores in Canada, U.S. and Britain.

9

American **Pete Sampras**, 28, captures the Men's Singles title at Wimbledon with a victory over Australian Pat Rafter. It is his record-tying 7th Wimbledon and record-breaking 13th Grand Slam title. Sampras breaks Australian legend Roy Emerson's record.

10

Major League Baseball Standings:
NL East: Atlanta holds a 3-game lead on NY
Central: St. Louis is 8 games up on Cincinnati
West: Arizona is up 3 1/2 over San Francisco
East: NY & Toronto are tied 2 1/2 games up on Boston
Central: Chicago is 10 1/2 games up on Cleveland
West: Seattle is 3 games up on Oakland

11

President Clinton opens a **Mideast Peace Summit** at Camp David with Israeli Prime Minister Ehud Barak and Palestinian leader Yasser Arafat.

The American League downs the National League 6-3 at the **MLB All-Star game** in Atlanta. The game MVP, Derek Jeter, goes 3 for 3 with 2 RBI and 1 run scored.

12

On the hit TV show **"Survivor"** housewife Gretchen Cordy is voted off the island.

The Russians launch the long-delayed 3rd module of the **International Space Station**, now under construction high above the Earth. The module named Zvezda (meaning "star") contains the living quarters for future crew members, along with the station's life support, flight, propulsion, power, and computer systems.

13

A **television news helicopter** captures videotape of a violent scuffle between Philadelphia, PA police officers and a man who had allegedly shot an officer and then stole a patrol car.

The #1 song on the Billboard Hot Country Singles Music Chart is **"I Hope You Dance"** by Lee Ann Womack with Sons of the Desert.

14

The largest punitive damages awarded in U.S. history is given by a Miami-Dade County Circuit Court jury of $144.8 billion to **Florida smokers** who claimed they had been harmed by cigarettes. The class-action lawsuit, launched against the tobacco companies some two years ago, was the first lawsuit filed on behalf of smokers to reach trial.

15

Santa Ana, California, collector Brian Siegel pays a record $1.27 million to the **eBay online** auction house for a 1909 American Tobacco Co. card depicting Hall of Fame Pittsburgh Pirate shortstop Honus Wagner. Chicago owner Michael Gidwitz had paid $640,500 for the card during 1996.

16

Michael Andretti captures his 6th career Molson Toronto Indy. Adrian Fernandez finishes second with Canadian Paul Tracy third. Andretti's 40th CART victory leaves him 27 wins shy of A.J. Foyt's Champ-Car record.

Legally blind **Marla Runyan** becomes the first blind athlete on a U.S. Olympic team, by placing third in the 1,500-meter race at the Olympic trials in Sacramento, California.

17

The West defeats the East 73-61 at the 2nd **WNBA All-Star game** in Phoenix, Arizona. Houston Comets' Tina Thompson is named as the game's MVP.

Marvel comic book superheros come to life in the film **"The X-Men"** directed by Bryan Singer. Wheelchair bound Patrick Stewart stars as "Professor X", leader of the good Guy Mutants who include Halle Berry, Hugh Jackman. Ian McKellen stars as the leader of the dark side in the movie released by 20th Century-Fox.

18

Chart Toppers:
The #1 song on the Billboard Hot 100 Singles Music Chart is **"Everything You Want"** by Vertical Horizon.

Charlie Sheen signs on to join the cast of the hit TV series "Spin City".

19

Russian President Vladimir Putin takes a trip to Communist North Korea, the first ever by a Russian President.

On the hit TV show **"Survivor"** tradesman Greg Buis is voted off the island.

20

NASA scientists warn that a warming climate is melting more than 50 billion tons (45 cubic km) of the Greenland ice sheet a year, adding about 22 cm of water to the overall global sea level.

Musician **Carlos Santana** turns 53.

21

Lance Armstrong of the U.S. averages 53.986 km per hour to win the 58.5-km individual time trial in the fastest race record at that distance in the 87-year history of the **Tour de France**. It is his first stage victory after building his way to the top over the previous 18 stages.

22

Some 13,000 fans answer a casting call at Harrison High School in New Jersey to appear on the popular HBO series **"The Sopranos"**. The hit TV series is about a fictional New Jersey mob family.

Miami, Fla.: WBA Super Welterweight champion **Felix Trinidad** successfully defends his title with a third-round TKO over France's Mamadou Thiam.

23

Tiger Woods, 24, wins the 129th British Open Golf Title at St. Andrews, Scotland, becoming the youngest golfer to have won all 4 majors.

Karrie Webb wins the 55th LPGA U.S. Women's Open in Gurnee, Illinois.

American **Lance Armstrong**, 28, wins his second consecutive *Tour de France* bicycle race.

24

For the first time in internet publishing, author **Stephen King** offers fans a chance to download the first chapter of his serial novel, "The Plant", for $1 per installment. King's recent novella, "Riding the Bullet", was electronically published in March by Simon & Schuster.

N.Y.C.'s Central Park is closed to spray for the **West Nile virus** that killed 7 people last year.

25

An **Air France Concorde**, carrying German tourists to N.Y.C. for a luxury cruise, crashes shortly after takeoff in Paris, killing 113 in the first-ever crash by a Concorde. All 109 aboard are killed along with 4 people in the hotel that the jet slams into.

The Camp David **Mideast Peace Talks** collapse in a deadlock over the future of Jerusalem.

26

On the hit TV show **"Survivor"** student Jenna Lewis is voted off the island. Only 7 survivors now remain.

VHI and Entertainment Weekly magazine list the Feb. 9th, 1964, appearance on "The Ed Sullivan Show" by **The Beatles** as TV's biggest *rock n' roll* moment. An estimated 73 million people watched the band from Liverpool perform that Sunday night in 1964.

27

Harrison Ford and Michelle Pfeiffer star in the new scary film **"What Lies Beneath"**. Robert Zemeckis directed the film which is released by DreamWorks Pictures.

Chart Toppers:
The #1 song on the Billboard Hot 100 Singles Music Chart is **"Beni"** by matchbox twenty.

28

Kathie Lee Gifford, 46, makes her final appearance on the hit live daytime talk show "Live with Regis & Kathie Lee". Gifford has decided to leave the show to pursue her acting and singing career. She was on the hit TV show for 15 years. Her first show appearance took place on June 24th, 1985.

29

Actor **Brad Pitt**, 36, marries actress **Jennifer Aniston**, 31, in Malibu Beach, California.

Former San Francisco 49ers Joe Montana, Ronnie Lott and Dave Wilcox, plus Oakland Raider Howie Long and Pittsburgh Steeler owner Dan Rooney, are inducted into the **Pro Football Hall of Fame** in Canton, Ohio.

30

Chart Toppers:
The #1 song on the Billboard Hot 100 Singles Music Chart is **"It's Gonna Be Me"** by 'N Sync.

Dorothy Delasin, 19, becomes the LPGA's youngest winner in 25 years, winning the *Giant Eagle LPGA Classic* in Warren, Ohio, over Pat Hurst in a play-off.

31

Comedian **Dennis Miller** joins Al Michaels and Dan Fouts on ABC Sports' Monday Night Football for the Hall of Fame Game. Miller has been added to the booth to help improve on last year's sliding ABC-TV ratings. Monday Night Football first made its debut in 1970.

Dorothy Delasin, 19, becomes the youngest winner on the LPGA Tour in 25 years. (See July 30th)

The Beatles appearance on "The Ed Sullivan Show" in 1964. (See July 26th)

Harrison Ford and Michelle Pfeiffer in a scene from the new film "What Lies Beneath" (See July 27th)

Tiger Woods wins the PGA Championship earning his third major golf title of the year.

SUNDAY	MONDAY	TUESDAY	WEDNESDAY	THURSDAY	FRIDAY	SATURDAY

Julie Krone (photo with Hall of Fame plaque)

Monday: The winningest female jockey in history, Julie Krone is inducted into the U.S. Racing Hall of Fame. (See August 7th)

Tuesday 1: The **world's tallest roller coaster**, the Nagashima Spaland's *Steel Dragon 2000*, opens at a Japanese amusement park. The 2.4 km ride scales a 320-foot hill then races down a 68-degree slope. The ride lasts nearly 4 minutes.

Darva Conger, who married Rick Rockwell on TV's "Who Wants to Marry A Multimillionaire", appears in the August issue of Playboy magazine.

Wednesday 2: On the hit TV show **"Survivor"** basketball coach Gervase Peterson is voted off the island.

The #1 album on the Billboard 200 Music Chart for the 10th consecutive week is **"The Marshall Mathers LP"** by Eminem.

Thursday 3: On the final night of the **Republican National Convention** in Philadelphia, Texas Governor George W. Bush accepts the party's nomination to run for President. On August 2nd, former Defense Secretary Richard B. Cheney accepted the nomination to be Bush's running mate.

Proud To Be A Republican

Friday 4: The **Queen Mother** celebrates her 100th birthday.

Old guys Clint Eastwood, Donald Sutherland, Tommy Lee Jones and James Garner are recruited by NASA in the new comedy film **"Space Cowboys"**, released by Warner Bros.

Kevin Bacon stars as a scientist who tests his own invisible formula, in the film **"Hollow Man"**.

Saturday 5: **"Yankee Paco"** becomes the first Canadian-sired horse to win the Hambletonian at the Meadowlands in East Rutherford, N.J. Driver Trevor Tichie wins the *Kentucky Derby* of trotting.

Legendary actor **Sir Alec Guinness**, 86, dies in England.

Bobby Labonte wins the NASCAR Brickyard 400 event.

Sunday 6: Canadian **Lori Kane**, 35, wins her first LPGA title with a 72-hole, 205 total, at the Michelob Light Classic at the Fox Run Golf Club in Eureka, Missouri. Kane picks up $120,000 for the victory.

Monday 7: Democratic U.S. Presidential hopeful Al Gore, 52, names **Sen. Joseph Lieberman**, 58, as his Vice-Presidential running mate. Lieberman is the first Jewish candidate ever on a major presidential ticket.

Proud To Be A Democrat

Former jockey **Julie Krone**, 37, becomes the first woman inducted into the U.S. Racing Hall of Fame in Saratoga Springs, N.Y.

Tuesday 8: Welsh actress **Catherine Zeta-Jones**, 30, gives birth to a son, Dylan Michael Douglas. Zeta-Jones is engaged to actor Michael Douglas, 55.

The #1 song on the Billboard Hot Country Singles Music Chart for the 5th consecutive week is **"I Hope You Dance"** by Lee Ann Womack with Sons of the Desert.

Wednesday 9: On the hit TV show **"Survivor"**, college student Colleen Haskell is voted off the island. There are now 5 survivors left.

Bowing to pressure, **Bridgestone/Firestone Inc.** announces it is recalling 6.5 million tires in Canada and the U.S. on sport utility vehicles and light trucks. The tires are being blamed for at least 46 deaths, caused by the tires shredding.

Thursday 10: **Chart Toppers:** The #1 song on the Billboard Hot 100 Singles Music Chart for the 2nd consecutive week is **"It's Gonna Be Me"** by 'N Sync.

Actors **Rosanna Arquette** and **Antonio Banderas** celebrate their 40th birthdays.

Friday 11: Keanu Reeves plays a quarterback in the new Warner Bros. film **"The Replacements"**, with co-star Gene Hackman as the coach.

Pop singer **Madonna** gives birth to a boy, Rocco Ritchie, at L.A.'s Cedars-Sinai Medical Center. The baby's father is British film director Guy Ritchie.

Saturday 12: Academy Award winner, **Loretta Young**, 87, dies of ovarian cancer in Los Angeles.

During the largest naval exercise in years by the Russian Northern Fleet, the 14,000-ton nuclear submarine **"Kursk"** sinks to the bottom in 108 meters of water in the Barents Sea. The crew of 118 are feared dead.

Sunday 13: **Evander Holyfield**, 37, wins the vacant WBA Heavyweight Boxing title with a unanimous 12-round decision over John Ruiz, in Las Vegas.

Kevin Zegers recruits a chimpanzee to help out his Little League Hockey team, in the new comedy film **"MVP: Most Valuable Primate"**. The movie co-stars Jamie Renee Smith.

Monday 14: **Chart Toppers:** The #1 song on the Billboard Hot 100 Singles Music Chart is **"Incomplete"** by Sisqo.

The #1 album on the Billboard 200 Music Chart for the 2nd consecutive week is **"Now 4"** by Various Artists.

Tuesday 15: An 83-year-old woman, **Tillie Totter**, is rescued after 3 days in a snake-infested swamp after her car plunged 40 feet off a bridge on Florida's Interstate 595.

Frank Gifford turns 70 and **Kathie Lee Gifford** turns 47.

Wednesday 16: On the hit TV show **"Survivor"**, neurologist Sean Kenniff is voted off the island.

The # song on the Billboard Hot Country Singles Music Chart is **"What About Now"** by Lonestar.

Thursday 17: VP **Al Gore** accepts the Democratic Party nomination for President on the final night of the party convention in Los Angeles. Senator Joseph Lieberman accepted the VP nomination yesterday. One of the more memorable moments of the convention occurs when Gore passionately kisses his wife Tipper, who praised him as a *"decisive leader with strong values"* during her introduction speech.

Friday 18: Jennifer Lopez stars as a scientist who gets inside the head of a serial killer, in the new film **"The Cell"**, with Vince Vaughn and Vincent D'Onofrio. The film is released by New Line Cinema.

In an AP poll the Nebraska Cornhuskers are the #1 ranked college football team going into this season. Florida State is ranked #2.

POLL

Saturday 19: The "N.Y. Times" reports that, for the first time in 50 million years, the thick ice that covers the **Arctic Ocean** at the North Pole has melted, leaving a mile-wide stretch of water.

Newsweek Presidential Poll:
Al Gore 48%
George Bush 42%

POLL

Sunday 20: **Tiger Woods**, 24, becomes the first golfer since Ben Hogan in 1953 to win 3 majors in one year, winning the 82nd PGA Championship over Bob May following a 3-hole play-off at the Valhalla Golf Club in Louisville, Kentucky.

Tennis star **Martina Hingis** wins the Du Maurier Open in Montreal over Serena Williams.

Monday 21: 86 major **wildfires** continue to burn in a dozen western states as more than 20,000 firefighters and some 3,000 military troops fight to stop the fires that have already charred more than a million acres.

British child-actor, **Daniel Radcliffe**, 11, is cast from the thousands of candidates in the starring role for the upcoming Warner Bros. film "Harry Potter and the Sorcerer's Stone."

Tuesday 22: The winners of the 23rd annual Kennedy Center Honors for **Lifetime Achievement in the Arts** are announced: Dancer Mikhail Baryshnikov, tenor Placido Domingo, actors Clint Eastwood and Angela Lansbury along with rock'n roller Chuck Berry. The honors gala event will be held December 3rd.

Wednesday 23: On the final show of TV's hit **"Survivor"**, corporate trainer Richard Hatch, 39, wins the vote and $1 million over Kelly Wiglesworth, who wins $100,000. Fan favorite Rudy was eliminated from the final vote by Wiglesworth who chose Hatch. Earlier Wiglesworth won the *immunity challenge* over Rudy when he absentmindedly dropped his hand from the wooden pole. The final episode of "Survivor" was watched by an estimated 51 million viewers.

Thursday 24: Mattel has launched the **Olympic Fan Barbie Doll** ($17.50) complete with various team colors including Australia, Canada, Spain and France. Also available is the Paralympic Champion **"Becky"**, which comes with a wheelchair, water bottle and helmet ($26).

Friday 25: Universal/Beacon releases the high school cheerleading film, **"Bring It On"**, with Kirsten Dunst as the new team captain. Jesse Bradford co-stars in the new film directed by Peyton Reed.

Buena Vista releases a new comedy film about 4 over-the-hill wise guys who miss their old ways, in **"The Crew"**, starring Richard Dreyfuss, Burt Reynolds, Seymour Cassel and Dan Hedaya.

Saturday 26: Maracaibo, Venezuela, defeats Bellaire, Texas, 3-2 to win the **Little League Baseball World Series** in Williamsport, Pennsylvania.

League MVP and leading scorer Sheryl Swoopes scores 31 points, and Cynthia Cooper adds 25, to lead the Houston Comets to a 79-73 victory over the NY Liberty to capture the **WNBA championship** for the 4th consecutive year. Cooper is named the series MVP for the 4th year.

Sunday 27: A fire breaks out in the upper reaches of the world's 2nd tallest structure, the 1,772-foot **Ostankino Television Tower** in Moscow. 4 people are killed. The fire burns for 26 hours.

Tiger Woods shoots a tournament record 21-under-par 259 to capture the NEC Invitational at the Firestone Country Club in Akron, Ohio. It is Woods' lowest 72-hole score of his professional career. Justin Leonard finishes second.

Monday 28: The 100th **U.S. Amateur Golf Championship** in Springfield, New Jersey, is won by Jeff Quinney, 21, in a play-off over James Driscoll, on the Upper Course at Baltusrol Golf Course.

The **word "rats"** appears for a split second during a television commercial for Texas Gov. George W. Bush, as he critiques the Medicare prescription drug plan put forth by VP Al Gore.

Tuesday 29: While preparing a **giant cod** for market at an Australian fish wholesaler, workers find the remains of a human head inside.

As **temperatures in northern Texas** reach 102°F, the area breaks a record, going 60 days without moisture, breaking the dry spell record set during the Dust Bowl days of the Depression.

Wednesday 30: Se Ri Pak, 22, of South Korea collects $117,500 from the $225,000 purse at the inaugural **Lorie Kane Island Challenge** Women's Golf Skins event in Roseneath, P.E.I. The first pro event of its kind to be held in Canada also features LPGA members Annika Sorenstam, Nancy Lopez and host Lorie Kane.

Thursday 31: The #1 album on the Billboard 200 Music Chart is **"Country Grammar"** by Nelly.

TV Programs Tonight On NBC:
8:00 Friends
8:30 Will & Grace
9:00 Will & Grace
9:30 Just Shoot Me
10:00 ER

2000 GMC Aztec with tent out.

The final four of the hit television series "Survivor":
Kelly Wiglesworth,
Sue Hawk, Richard Hatch and
Ex-Navy Seal Rudy Boesch.
(See August 23rd)

(Photo credit CBS Photo Archive)

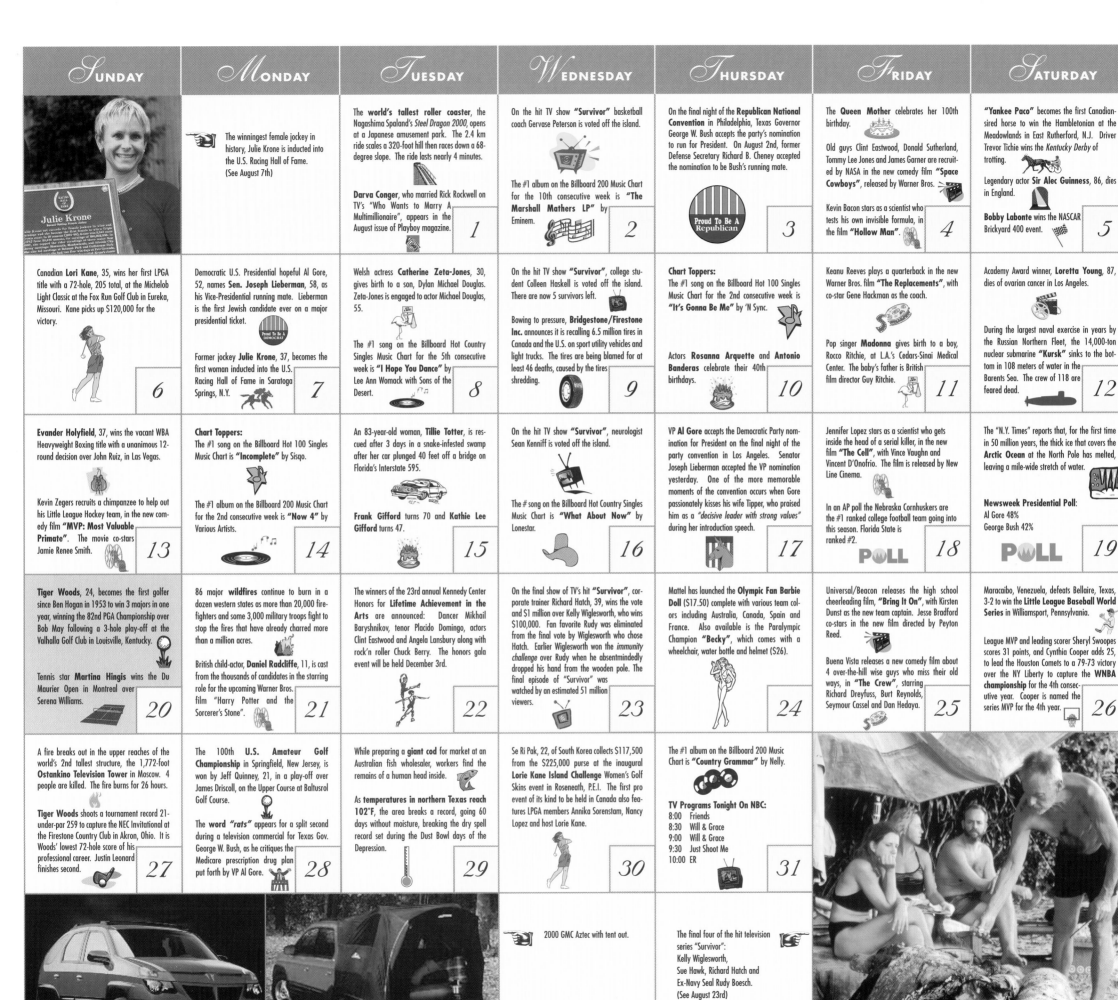

U.S. Track and Field star Marion Jones captures 5 Olympic Medals in Sydney, Australia.

Sunday	Monday	Tuesday	Wednesday	Thursday	Friday	Saturday

The U.S. Consumer Product Safety Commission reports that more than 9,400 Americans (90% under the age of 15) have reported to hospital emergency rooms this year as a result of injuries incurred while using scooters which have had a resurgance in popularity this year.

Patrick Fugit and Kate Hudson on the "Almost Famous" tour '73. (See September 20th)

1

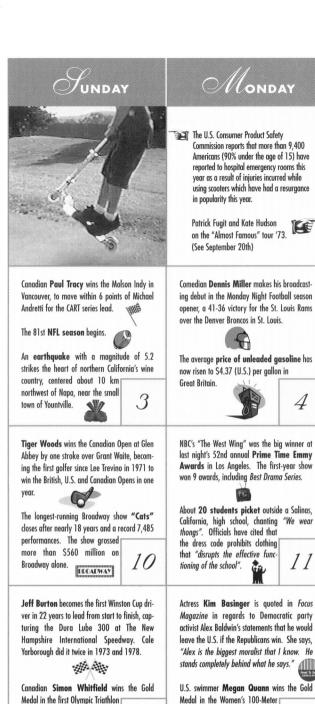

Elian Gonzalez returns to school in Cardenas, Cuba, having been kept out of the public eye since his return home last June.

In an effort to raise cash for a social welfare system, China launches its first **nationwide lottery**. A 24¢ ticket is good for all 15 draws for a chance to win the top prize of $120,000.

2

Pop singer **Brian Littrell**, 25, of The Backstreet Boys, marries Leighanne Wallace, 31, in Atlanta, Georgia. Wallace was an extra on the 1997 video "As Long As You Love Me". Group member Kevin Richardson also married earlier this year.

The #1 song on the Billboard Hot Country Singles Music Chart for the 4th consecutive week is **"What About Me"** by Lonestar.

3

Canadian **Paul Tracy** wins the Molson Indy in Vancouver, to move within 6 points of Michael Andretti for the CART series lead.

The 81st **NFL season** begins.

An **earthquake** with a magnitude of 5.2 strikes the heart of northern California's wine country, centered about 10 km northwest of Napa, near the small town of Yountville.

4

Comedian **Dennis Miller** makes his broadcasting debut in the Monday Night Football season opener, a 41-36 victory for the St. Louis Rams over the Denver Broncos in St. Louis.

The average **price of unleaded gasoline** has now risen to $4.37 (U.S.) per gallon in Great Britain.

5

The **Best-Selling General Hardback Books** at this time are:
1) "Who Moved My Cheese?" by Spencer Johnson
2) "Body for Life" by Bill Phillips and Michael D'Orso
3) "Tuesdays with Morrie" by Mitch Albom
4) "It's Not About the Bike" by Lance Armstrong with Sally Jenkins

Actress **Raquel Welch** turns 60.

6

Canadian Prime Minister Jean Chrétien scolds the U.S. at the opening of U.N. Millennium Summit in New York for not paying $1.7 billion in back dues owed to the U.N., saying, *"We pay our bill at the first of the month. They don't. They should pay. We all pay".*

Margaret Salinger's memoirs, **"Dreamcatcher"** goes on sale in the U.S. She is the daughter of J.D. Salinger, 81, who wrote "The Catcher in the Rye".

7

Chart Toppers:
The #1 song on the Billboard Hot 100 Singles Music Chart for the 2nd consecutive week is **"Doesn't Really Matter"** by Janet.

American archaeologist **Arthur Demarest** announces the discovery of a large, well-preserved, 8th Century A.D. Mayan palace in a remote Guatemalan jungle.

8

The **space shuttle "Atlantis"**, with a crew of 5 astronauts and 2 cosmonauts aboard, launches from Cape Canaveral, Florida, for a planned rendezvous with the International Space Station. The supply ship is carrying thousands of pounds of equipment (including toilet paper) needed by the future inhabitants of the station.

9

Venus Williams wins the Women's U.S. Open Tennis title with a 6-4, 7-5 victory over Lindsay Davenport. Many are calling the match the hardest-hitting women's final in U.S. Open history. Tomorrow, Russia's Marat Safin, 20, will win his first Grand Slam Singles title with a 6-4, 6-3, 6-3 victory over Pete Sampras.

The #1 song on the Billboard Hot Country Singles Music Chart is **"It Must Be Love"** by Alan Jackson.

10

Tiger Woods wins the Canadian Open at Glen Abbey by one stroke over Grant Waite, becoming the first golfer since Lee Trevino in 1971 to win the British, U.S. and Canadian Opens in one year.

The longest-running Broadway show **"Cats"** closes after nearly 18 years and a record 7,485 performances. The show grossed more than $560 million on Broadway alone.

11

NBC's "The West Wing" was the big winner at last night's 52nd annual **Prime Time Emmy Awards** in Los Angeles. The first-year show won 9 awards, including *Best Drama Series.*

About **20 students picket** outside a Salinas, California, high school, chanting *"We wear thongs".* Officials have cited that the dress code prohibits clothing that *"disrupts the effective functioning of the school".*

12

Two days after Indiana University fired controversial basketball coach **Bobby Knight** for repeated misconduct, the University hires assistant Mike Davis as interim coach. John Treolar is appointed as interim associate coach. The players had told the school's athletic director that they would defect en masse if Davis or Treolar were not hired.

13

The inaugural **Latin Grammy Awards** take place in L.A., California, and are broadcast to more than 120 countries worldwide. Ricky Martin opens the telecast with a tribute to the late *Mambo King,* **Tito Puente**, who died on May 31st.

The Canadian edition of the hit TV show **"Who Wants To Be A Millionaire"** debuts at 8 pm with host Pamela Wallin.

14

Morgan Freeman stars in the new twisted comedy **"Nurse Betty"**, released by USA Films, and starring Renee Zellweger, Greg Kinnear and Chris Rock.

The #1 song on the Billboard Hot Country Singles Music Chart is **"It Must Be Love"** by Alan Jackson.

15

The **XXVII Summer Olympic Games** get under way with the lighting of the Olympic torch by Cathy Freeman, before a crowd of 110,000 at the Olympic Stadium in Sydney, Australia. More than 10,000 athletes from 200 countries will compete for glory over the 16 days of events. Freeman, an Aboriginal Australian, will win the Gold Medal in the Women's 400-Meters Track & Field event on Sept. 25th.

16

Australian swimmer **Ian Thorpe**, 17, sets a world record in the Men's 400-Meter Freestyle. Thorpe, known as the *"Thorpedo",* will go on to win two more Gold Medals with the relay team in the 400 and 800 Meter Freestyle Relays. He will also win Silver medals in the 200-Meter Freestyle and the 400-Meter Medley Relay.

17

Jeff Burton becomes the first Winston Cup driver in 22 years to lead from start to finish, capturing the Dura Lube 300 at The New Hampshire International Speedway. Cale Yarborough did it twice in 1973 and 1978.

Canadian **Simon Whitfield** wins the Gold Medal in the first Olympic Triathlon event.

18

Actress **Kim Basinger** is quoted in *Focus Magazine* in regards to Democratic party activist Alex Baldwin's statements that he would leave the U.S. if the Republicans win. She says, *"Alex is the biggest moralist that I know. He stands completely behind what he says."*

U.S. swimmer **Megan Quann** wins the Gold Medal in the Women's 100-Meter Breaststroke.

19

In what could be the biggest step in **U.S-China relations** since President Nixon's 1972 visit to the Great Wall, the U.S. Senate votes 83-15 to permanently normalize trade with China.

20

Patrick Fugit stars as a 15-year-old writer who tours with a 1970's band called "Still Water" so he can get a story for "Rolling Stone Magazine", in the new film **"Almost Famous"**, with Kate Hudson, Frances McDormand and Billy Crudup. Director Cameron Crowe wrote the screenplay about his experiences as a young Rolling Stone writer. The movie is released by DreamWorks. Crowe will win an Oscar for his *Original Screenplay.*

21

U.S. swimmer **Lenny Krayzelburg** wins his second Gold medal of the games with an Olympic record time in the 200m backstroke. He won the 100m Backstroke on Sept. 18 will win a third Gold Medal in the 400m Medley Relay on Sept. 23rd. U.S. teammates Dara Torres and Jenny Thompson tie for Bronze medals in the Women's 100m freestyle. Torres will capture 2 Relay Gold Medals and 3 Bronze Medals in total. Thompson will lead the relay team to 3 Gold Medals.

22

President Clinton orders the release of 30-million barrels of oil from American emergency stockpiles in a move to ease soaring oil prices that rose to a high of nearly $38 earlier this week.

American swimmer **Brooke Bennett** wins the Gold Medal, with a new Olympic record, in the Women's 800m Freestyle. Bennett also set an Olympic record on Sept. 17th in the 400m Freestyle.

23

Marion Jones, 24, of the U.S. wins an Olympic Gold Medal in the 100-Meter Sprint with a time of 10.75 seconds. Jones will go on to become the first woman to win 5 medals in Track and Field in a single Olympic games: 200m Gold; Long Jump Bronze; anchor in the 4x100m Relay Team Gold; 3rd on the 4x400m Relay Team Gold.

Maurice Greene of the U.S. wins Gold in the Men's 100m sprint.

24

Even a spin-out in his Ferrari with 4 laps to go can't keep **Michael Schumacher** from winning the inaugural U.S. Grand Prix, run at the Indianapolis Motor Speedway.

Laura Wilkinson of the U.S. wins the Gold Medal in Women's Platform Diving. Canada's Anne Montminy wins the Bronze.

25

Boston Bruin enforcer **Marty McSorley's** trial opens in Vancouver for his stick-swinging assault on Vancouver Canuck tough-guy Donald Brasher on Feb. 21st in Vancouver. McSorley pleads not guilty, saying the hit was an accident. He will be found guilty and receive an 18-month conditional discharge.

Canada's Olympic **Men's Basketball team** upsets defending World Champion Yugoslavia, 83-75.

26

The **U.S. Women's softball team**, managed by Sparky Anderson, wins the Olympic Gold medal with a 2-1 victory in 8 innings over Japan.

Emmy award-winning actor **Richard Mulligan**, 67, dies after a long battle with cancer. Mulligan is best known for his roles in the television sitcoms "Soap" and "Empty Nest".

27

The Canadian **tennis team** of Daniel Nestor and Sebastien Lareau upsets "the Woodies", Australians Mark Woodforde and Todd Woodbridge, to win the Gold Medal in Men's Doubles. The defending Olympic champions from Australia will retire from professional tennis following this match. The Women's Doubles Gold Medal will be won Sept. 28th by sisters Venus & Serena Williams from the U.S.

28

Canadians and world leaders mourn the death of former Canadian Prime Minister **Pierre Elliott Trudeau**, who led the nation from 1968-1979 and again from 1980-1984. In 1998 Trudeau lost his son Michel who died suddenly in an avalanche in British Columbia. He is survived by his two other sons Justin and Sasha, and his ex-wife Margaret Trudeau.

29

The CBS-TV reality show **"Big Brother"** comes to an end after 88-days as Eddie McGee, a one-legged New Yorker, wins the $500,000 first -place prize.

Buena Vista releases the film **"Remember the Titans"**, starring Denzel Washington and Will Patton as football coaches at a forced-integration school.

30

In the **bloodiest clashes** in the West Bank and Gaza Strip since 1996, 12 rock-throwing Palestinians are killed when Israeli troops fire back. Among the dead is a 12-year-old boy caught in the crossfire.

Tennis star **Pete Sampras** marries former Miss Teen U.S.A. (1990), actress Bridgette Wilson, 27, at his home in Beverly Hills, California.

Olympic Triathlon Gold Medal winner, Canadian Simon Whitfield. (See September 17th)

Aboriginal Australian Cathy Freeman lights the Olympic Torch and parades around the Olympic Stadium after winning a Gold Medal in the Women's 400-Meter Race. (See September 15th)

Australia's Ian Thorpe holds up the Olympic Gold Medal he won in the 400-Meter Freestyle Swimming event. (See September 16th)

New TV sitcom stars Tom Cavanagh in "Ed", and Bette Midler in "Bette".

SUNDAY	MONDAY	TUESDAY	WEDNESDAY	THURSDAY	FRIDAY	SATURDAY
Major League Baseball season leaders: Batting: AL - Nomar Garciaparra (Boston) .372 NL - Todd Helton (Colorado) .372 RBI's: AL - Edgar Martinez (Seattle) 145 NL - Todd Helton (Colorado) 147 HR: AL - Troy Glaus (Anaheim) 47 NL - Sammy Sosa (Chicago) 50 The SF Giants finish with the best overall record with 97 wins and 65 losses. **1**	The **Summer Olympics** conclude in Sydney, Australia, with the U.S. winning 39 Gold, 25 Silver and 33 Bronze. Russia places second with 32 Gold, 28 Silver and 28 Bronze. China finishes third with 28 Gold, 16 Silver and 15 Bronze. Fifty-one beefy studs from across the U.S. strut their stuff on the FOX-TV Network special **"The Sexiest Bachelor in America Pageant"**, airing at 8:00 pm. **2**	John Lennon's murderer, **Mark David Chapman** is refused parole by New York State officials. FOX-TV premieres a new sci-fi drama, **"Dark Angel"**, starring Jessica Alba, 19, as a genetically-enhanced kick-butt avenger. Created by director James Cameron, the series, set in 21st-century Seattle, co-stars Michael Weatherly and John Savage. **3**	Canadian **Shania Twain** wins the *Entertainer of the Year* Award at the Country Music Association Awards at the Grand Ole Opry in Nashville, Tennessee. NBC-TV premieres Aaron Spelling's **"Titans"**, starring Yasmine Bleeth, Perry King and Victoria Principal. **4**	The new authorized book **"The Beatles Anthology"** by The Beatles is released. WB-TV premieres the new show **"Gilmore Girls"**, starring Lauren Graham as a single mom and her teenage daughter played by Alexis Bledel. CBS-TV premieres the animated comedy series **"Palswick"** and **"Our Hero"**. **5**	CBS-TV premieres a new drama series, **"The Fugitive"**, based on the classic 1960's TV series about a man wrongfully convicted of killing his wife. Tim Daly stars as "Dr. Richard Kimble" with Mykelti Williamson as his relentless pursuer "Lt. Philip Gerard". CBS-TV premieres **"CSI: Crime Scene Investigation"**. William Petersen and Marg Helgenberger star as crime scene investigators. **6**	The new **Columbus Blue Jackets** lose their first regular-season NHL game 5-3 to the Chicago Black Hawks, at the Nationwide Arena in Columbus, Ohio. The **Minnesota Wild** lost their first game in the big leagues, 3-1, to the Mighty Ducks in Anaheim yesterday. CBS-TV premieres **"That's Life"**, starring Heather Paige Kent as a waitress who heads back to school. The series also stars Debi Mazar, Ellen Burstyn and Paul Sorvino. **7**
NBC-TV premieres **"Ed"**, starring Tom Cavanagh as a N.Y. lawyer who returns to his hometown of Stuckeyville, Ohio, and buys the bowling alley. The series co-stars include Julie Bowen, Josh Randall & Jana Marie Hupp. **Michael Schumacher**, driving his Ferrari, clinches the Formula One title with a victory at the Japanese Grand Prix at the Suzuka Circuit. **8**	Ben Stiller meets the wacky dad (Robert De Niro) of his girlfriend, Teri Polo, in the new comedy film, **"Meet The Parents"**, with Blythe Danner as the mother. Directed by Jay Roach, the film is released by Universal. Joel Schumacher directs the story of a Vietnam training camp in the swamps of Louisiana in the new film **"Tigerland"**, starring Colin Farrell and Matthew Davis. **9**	American Jack Kilby, 77, of Texas Instruments, who played a vital scientific role in the invention of the computer chip, is awarded a **Nobel Prize in Physics**. Kilby shares the honor with Zhores Alferov of Russia, and Herbert Kroemer of Germany. ABC-TV premieres **"The Geena Davis Show"** and its new medical drama **"Gideon's Crossing"**. **10**	CBS-TV premieres the new sitcom **"Bette"**, starring Bette Midler, 54, with Kevin Dunn as her husband **"Roy"**. The 100th mission in the U.S. shuttle program gets underway with the launch of the **"Discovery Orbiter"** from Cape Canaveral, Florida. **11**	Aden, Yemen: Two suicide bombers in a small boat attack the navy destroyer **"U.S.S. Cole"**, killing 6 American sailors with an additional 11 others missing and presumed dead. The bomb, estimated at 500 kilograms of TNT, also injures 35 sailors, including 5 who are listed as critical. President Clinton calls the attack a *"despicable and cowardly act"*. **12**	Jamie Bell, 14, stars as a coal miner's son who wants to give up boxing for ballet, in the new British film **"Billy Elliot"**. Julie Walters plays Billy's dance teacher in this uplifting movie saga released by Universal. DreamWorks releases the new political film drama **"The Contender"**, starring Joan Allen, Jeff Bridges, Gary Oldman and Sam Elliott. **13**	South Korean President **Kim Dae-Jung**, 75, is announced as the winner of the Nobel Peace Prize. In proclaiming the award, the Norwegian Nobel committee cited Dae-Jung's work for civil rights and democracy. Dae-Jung has *"attempted to overcome more than 50 years of war and hostility between North and South Korea"*. **Angela Perez Baraquio**, 24, is crowned as the new *Miss America* in Atlantic City, New Jersey. **14**
Buddy Lazier places fourth at the *Excite 500* in Fort Worth, Texas, to clinch his first Indy title. Scott Goodyear wins the race and finishes second overall. **Dale Earnhardt** wins the *Winston 500* at Talladega Superspeedway in Alabama. Richard Gere plays a gynecologist in the new Robert Altman film **"Dr. T & The Women"**, co-starring Helen Hunt and Farrah Fawcett. The film is released by Artisan. **15**	The **NY Mets**, led by ace left-handed pitcher Mike Hampton, defeat the visiting St. Louis Cardinals 7-0, to win the NLCS in 5 games. Hampton is chosen as the NLCS **MVP**. The **NY Yankees** will clinch the ALCS on Oct. 17th over Seattle in game 6. Pitcher Orlando (El Duque) Hernandez will be named as the series **MVP**. **16**	Colorado Avalanche goaltender **Patrick Roy** celebrates his NHL record-setting 448th career victory with a 4-3 overtime win over the Capitals in Washington. Roy passes Terry Sawchuk as the winningest NHL goalie. Pop star **George Michael** pays $2.1 million at auction for John Lennon's piano, on which Lennon composed the song "Imagine". **17**	Minus star Michael J. Fox, ABC's "Spin City" returns for a fifth season. The season premiere titled **"Hello Charlie"** marks the arrival of **Charlie Sheen**, 35, as the new deputy mayor "Charlie Crawford". **Macaulay Caulkin** stars as a 15-year-old boy seduced by his French teacher in the new Richard Nelson play "Madame Melville", at the Vaudeville Theatre in London. **18**	The Neil Simon comedy **"The Dinner Party"** opens at the Music Box Theater in New York City. John Ritter, Henry Winkler, Len Cariou, Jan Maxwell, Penny Fuller and Veanne Cox play three men and three women mysteriously summoned to dine at a posh hotel in Paris. **BROADWAY** **19**	20th Century-Fox releases the Harold Ramis film remake of the Faustian romantic comedy **"Bedazzled"**, starring Brendan Fraser and Elizabeth Hurley as the *Devil*. Warner Bros. releases **"Pay It Forward"**, starring Haley Joel Osment as a grade 7 student who comes up with a unique way of helping others. The film co-stars Kevin Spacey and Helen Hunt. **20**	Yankee second-baseman **Jose Vizcaino** records his 4th hit in game one of the World Series, driving in the winning run in the 12th inning, as the Yankees down the visiting NY Mets 4-3 in the longest series game (4 hrs., 51 min.) in history. **Chart Toppers:** The #1 song on the Billboard Hot 100 Singles Music Chart for the 2nd consecutive week is **"Come On Over Baby (All I Want Is You)"** by Christina Aguilera. **21**
The **NY Yankees** win game 2 of the World Series over the NY Mets 6-5. Derek Jeter, Tino Martinez and Paul O'Neill lead the way for the Yankees with 3 hits apiece. Winning pitcher Roger Clemens tosses the broken end of Mets catcher Mike Piazza's bat back at him as he trots to first base. Clemens will later be fined $50,000 by the MLB for his actions. **22**	FOX-TV premieres the new drama series set in a high school, **"Boston Public"**, starring Anthony Heald, Jessalyn Gilsig and Chi McBride. The show is written and produced by David E. Kelley. The #1 song on the Billboard Hot Country Singles Music Chart for the 3rd consecutive week is **"Kiss This"** by Aaron Tippin. **23**	Shea Stadium: The NY Mets defeat the visiting NY Yankees 4-2 in game three of the **"Subway Series"**. The Mets defeat Yankee starter Orlando (El Duque) Hernandez for his first career post-season loss, having gone 8-0 since 1998. The victory also ends the Yankees record steak of 14 straight World Series victories. NBC-TV premieres the **"Michael Richards Show"**, starring Richards as a bumbling detective. **24**	Wrestling fans can now buy stocks in their favorite pastime, as stock in **World Wrestling Federation Entertainment** begins trading on the New York City Stock Exchange. The visiting **NY Yankees**, led by Derek Jeter, defeat the NY Mets 3-2, to take a commanding 3-1 World Series lead. Jeter, who homered on the first pitch of the game, also tripled and scored two runs for the victors. **25**	The NY Yankees win their third consecutive **World Series** crown with a 4-2 win over the NY Mets at Shea Stadium. Yankee shortstop Derek Jeter, who batted .409 with two home runs, is named as the series *Most Valuable Player*. Jeter also extended his World Series hitting steak to 14 games. NBC-TV premieres **"Cursed"**, starring Steven Weber, Amy Pietz, Wendell Pierce and Chris Elliott. **26**	John Travolta and Lisa Kudrow team up to rig the local lottery in **"Lucky Numbers"**. Directed by Nora Ephron, the comedy film is released by Paramount Pictures. The Blair County witch is back and she's mad, in the new film **"Book of Shadows: Blair Witch 2"**, starring Jeffrey Donovan and Erica Leerhsen. The film is released by Artisan. **27**	CART driver **Gil de Ferran** posts the fastest lap in closed-course history at 241.428 mph in his Marlboro Honda Reynard, to win the pole for the *Marlboro 500* at the California Speedway in Fontana, California. de Ferran will finish fourth in the race, clinching the CART championship Vanderbilt trophy. Adrian Fernandez finishes second overall in the closest points race in CART history. **28**
The **Best-Selling Albums** at this time are: 1) "Rule" by Ja Rule 2) "Country Grammar" by Nelly 3) "Let's Get Ready" by Mystikal 4) "Human Clay" by Creed 5) "Revelation" by 98 Degrees The #1 song on the Billboard Hot Country Singles Music Chart is **"The Little Girl"** by John Michael Montgomery. **29**	TV comedian **Steve Allen**, 78, dies of an apparent heart attack at the home of his son in Encino, California. Allen, pioneer of the original "Tonight Show" (1953), also wrote more than 4,000 songs and 40 books during his illustrious career. **30**	U2's new CD, **"All That You Can't Leave Behind"** hits stores. The **50th NBA season** gets underway. A **Singapore Airlines** jumbo jet, taking off for Los Angeles, slams into an object on the runway and bursts into flames. The actual number of casualties is questionable. **31**				

John Savage, Jessica Alba and Michael Weatherly star in the new TV series "Dark Angel". (See October 3rd)

The cast of the new TV Drama Series "CSI: Crime Scene Investigation". (See October 6th)

(Far Right) The NY Yankees celebrate their World Series win. (See October 26th)

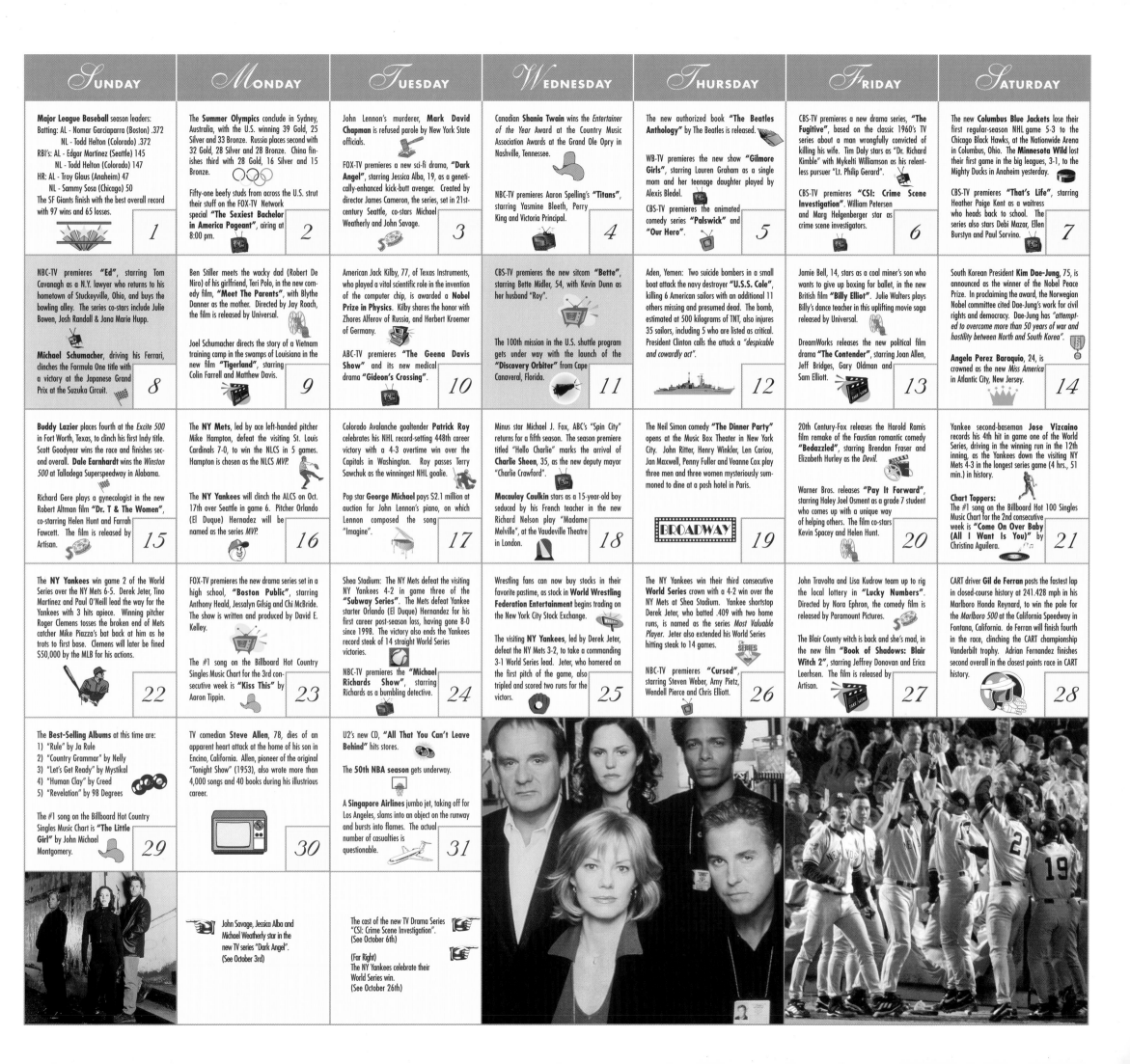

And....the new President-elect is....?

Sunday	Monday	Tuesday	Wednesday	Thursday	Friday	Saturday

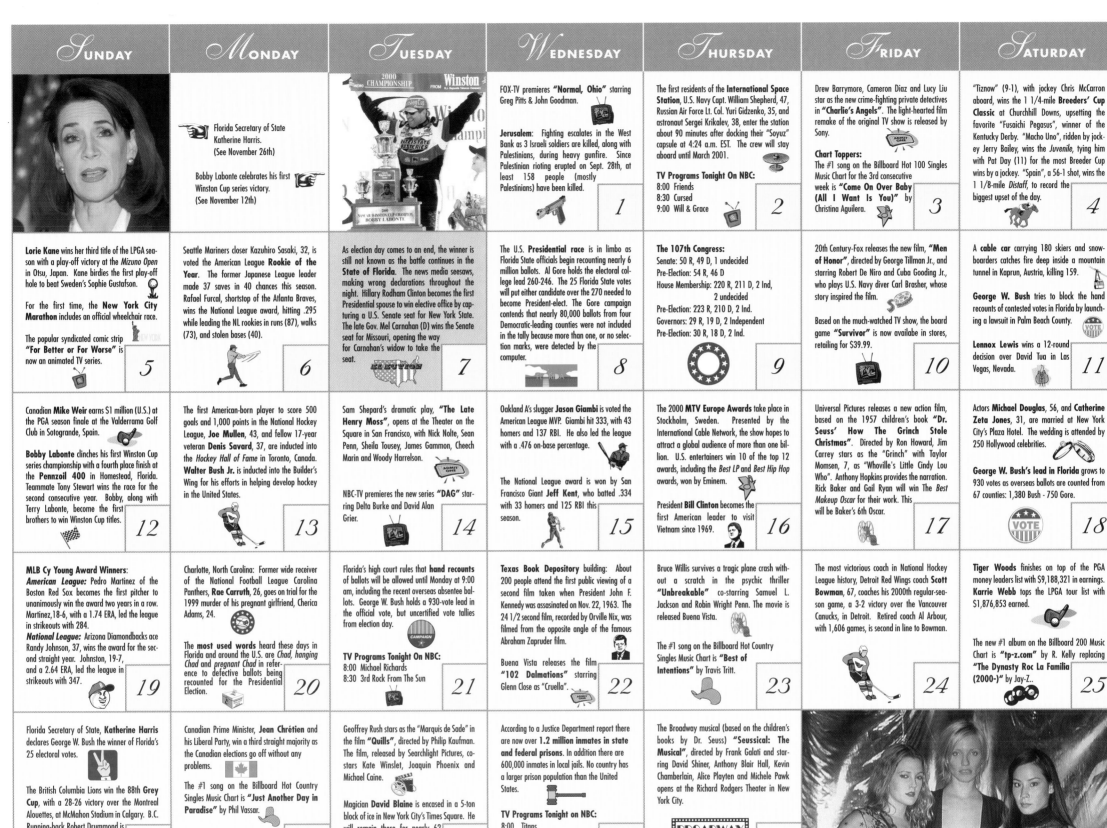

Florida Secretary of State Katherine Harris. (See November 26th)

Bobby Labonte celebrates his first Winston Cup series victory. (See November 12th)

1
FOX-TV premieres **"Normal, Ohio"** starring Greg Pitts & John Goodman.

Jerusalem: Fighting escalates in the West Bank as 3 Israeli soldiers are killed, along with Palestinians, during heavy gunfire. Since Palestinian rioting erupted on Sept. 28th, at least 158 people (mostly Palestinians) have been killed.

2
The first residents of the **International Space Station**, U.S. Navy Capt. William Shepherd, 47, Russian Air Force Lt. Col. Yuri Gidzenko, 35, and astronaut Sergei Krikalev, 38, enter the station about 90 minutes after docking their "Soyuz" capsule at 4:24 a.m. EST. The crew will stay aboard until March 2001.

TV Programs Tonight On NBC:
8:00 Friends
8:30 Cursed
9:00 Will & Grace

3
Drew Barrymore, Cameron Diaz and Lucy Liu star as the new crime-fighting private detectives in **"Charlie's Angels"**. The light-hearted film remake of the original TV show is released by Sony.

Chart Toppers:
The #1 song on the Billboard Hot 100 Singles Music Chart for the 3rd consecutive week is **"Come On Over Baby (All I Want Is You)"** by Christina Aguilera.

4
"Tiznow" (9-1), with jockey Chris McCarron aboard, wins the 1 1/4-mile **Breeders' Cup Classic** at Churchhill Downs, upsetting the favorite "Fusaichi Pegasus", winner of the Kentucky Derby. "Macho Uno", ridden by jockey Jerry Bailey, wins the *Juvenile*, tying him with Pat Day (11) for the most Breeder Cup wins by a jockey. "Spain", a 56-1 shot, wins the 1 1/8-mile *Distaff*, to record the biggest upset of the day.

5
Lorie Kane wins her third title of the LPGA season with a play-off victory at the *Mizuno Open* in Otsu, Japan. Kane birdies the first play-off hole to beat Sweden's Sophie Gustafson.

For the first time, the **New York City Marathon** includes an official wheelchair race.

The popular syndicated comic strip **"For Better or For Worse"** is now an animated TV series.

6
Seattle Mariners closer Kazuhiro Sasaki, 32, is voted the American League **Rookie of the Year**. The former Japanese League leader made 37 saves in 40 chances this season. Rafael Furcal, shortstop of the Atlanta Braves, wins the National League award, hitting .295 while leading the NL rookies in runs (87), walks (73), and stolen bases (40).

7
As election day comes to an end, the winner is still not known as the battle continues in the **State of Florida**. The news media seesaws, making wrong declarations throughout the night. Hillary Rodham Clinton becomes the first Presidential spouse to win elective office by capturing a U.S. Senate seat for New York State. The late Gov. Mel Carnahan (D) wins the Senate seat for Missouri, opening the way for Carnahan's widow to take the seat.

8
The U.S. **Presidential race** is in limbo as Florida State officials begin recounting nearly 6 million ballots. Al Gore holds the electoral college lead 260-246. The 25 Florida State votes will put either candidate over the 270 needed to become President-elect. The Gore campaign contends that nearly 80,000 ballots from four Democratic-leading counties were not included in the tally because more than one, or no selection marks, were detected by the computer.

9
The 107th Congress:
Senate: 50 R, 49 D, 1 undecided
Pre-Election: 54 R, 46 D
House Membership: 220 R, 211 D, 2 Ind, 2 undecided
Pre-Election: 223 R, 210 D, 2 Ind.
Governors: 29 R, 19 D, 2 Independent
Pre-Election: 30 R, 18 D, 2 Ind.

10
20th Century-Fox releases the new film, **"Men of Honor"**, directed by George Tillman Jr., and starring Robert De Niro and Cuba Gooding Jr., who plays U.S. Navy diver Carl Brasher, whose story inspired the film.

Based on the much-watched TV show, the board game **"Survivor"** is now availabe in stores, retailing for $39.99.

11
A **cable car** carrying 180 skiers and snowboarders catches fire deep inside a mountain tunnel in Kaprun, Austria, killing 159.

George W. Bush tries to block the hand recounts of contested votes in Florida by launching a lawsuit in Palm Beach County.

Lennox Lewis wins a 12-round decision over David Tua in Las Vegas, Nevada.

12
Canadian **Mike Weir** earns $1 million (U.S.) at the PGA season finale at the Valderrama Golf Club in Sotogrande, Spain.

Bobby Labonte clinches his first Winston Cup series championship with a fourth place finish at the **Pennzoil 400** in Homestead, Florida. Teammate Tony Stewart wins the race for the second consecutive year. Bobby, along with Terry Labonte, become the first brothers to win Winston Cup titles.

13
The first American-born player to score 500 goals and 1,000 points in the National Hockey League, **Joe Mullen**, 43, and fellow 17-year veteran **Denis Savard**, 37, are inducted into the *Hockey Hall of Fame* in Toronto, Canada. **Walter Bush Jr.** is inducted into the Builder's Wing for his efforts in helping develop hockey in the United States.

14
Sam Shepard's dramatic play, **"The Late Henry Moss"**, opens at the Theater on the Square in San Francisco, with Nick Nolte, Sean Penn, Sheila Tousey, James Gammon, Cheech Marin and Woody Harrelson.

NBC-TV premieres the new series **"DAG"** starring Delta Burke and David Alan Grier.

15
Oakland A's slugger **Jason Giambi** is voted the American League MVP. Giambi hit 333, with 43 homers and 137 RBI. He also led the league with a .476 on-base percentage.

The National League award is won by San Francisco Giant **Jeff Kent**, who batted .334 with 33 homers and 125 RBI this season.

16
The 2000 **MTV Europe Awards** take place in Stockholm, Sweden. Presented by the International Cable Network, the show hopes to attract a global audience of more than one billion. U.S. entertainers win 10 of the top 12 awards, including the *Best LP* and *Best Hip Hop* awards, won by Eminem.

President **Bill Clinton** becomes the first American leader to visit Vietnam since 1969.

17
Universal Pictures releases a new action film, based on the 1957 children's book **"Dr. Seuss' How The Grinch Stole Christmas"**. Directed by Ron Howard, Jim Carrey stars as the "Grinch" with Taylor Momsen, 7, as "Whoville's Little Cindy Lou Who". Anthony Hopkins provides the narration. Rick Baker and Gail Ryan will win The *Best Makeup Oscar* for their work. This will be Baker's 6th Oscar.

18
Actors **Michael Douglas**, 56, and **Catherine Zeta Jones**, 31, are married at New York City's Plaza Hotel. The wedding is attended by 250 Hollywood celebrities.

George W. Bush's lead in Florida grows to 930 votes as overseas ballots are counted from 67 counties: 1,380 Bush - 750 Gore.

19
MLB Cy Young Award Winners:
American League: Pedro Martinez of the Boston Red Sox becomes the first pitcher to unanimously win the award two years in a row. Martinez, 18-6, with a 1.74 ERA, led the league in strikeouts with 284.
National League: Arizona Diamondbacks ace Randy Johnson, 37, wins the award for the second straight year. Johnston, 19-7, and a 2.64 ERA, led the league in strikeouts with 347.

20
Charlotte, North Carolina: Former wide receiver of the National Football League Carolina Panthers, **Rae Carruth**, 26, goes on trial for the 1999 murder of his pregnant girlfriend, Cherica Adams, 24.

The **most used words** heard these days in Florida and around the U.S. are *Chad, hanging Chad* and *pregnant Chad* in reference to defective ballots being recounted for the Presidential Election.

21
Florida's high court rules that **hand recounts** of ballots will be allowed until Monday at 9:00 am, including the recent overseas absentee ballots. George W. Bush holds a 930-vote lead in the official vote, but uncertified vote tallies from election day.

TV Programs Tonight On NBC:
8:00 Michael Richards
8:30 3rd Rock From The Sun

22
Texas Book Depository building: About 200 people attend the first public viewing of a second film taken when President John F. Kennedy was assasinated on Nov. 22, 1963. The 24 1/2 second film, recorded by Orville Nix, was filmed from the opposite angle of the famous Abraham Zapruder film.

Buena Vista releases the film **"102 Dalmations"** starring Glenn Close as "Cruella".

23
Bruce Willis survives a tragic plane crash without a scratch in the psychic thriller **"Unbreakable"** co-starring Samuel L. Jackson and Robin Wright Penn. The movie is released Buena Vista.

The #1 song on the Billboard Hot Country Singles Music Chart is **"Best of Intentions"** by Travis Tritt.

24
The most victorious coach in National Hockey League history, Detroit Red Wings coach **Scott Bowman**, 67, coaches his 2000th regular-season game, a 3-2 victory over the Vancouver Canucks, in Detroit. Retired coach Al Arbour, with 1,606 games, is second in line to Bowman.

25
Tiger Woods finishes on top of the PGA money leaders list with $9,188,321 in earnings. **Karrie Webb** tops the LPGA tour list with $1,876,853 earned.

The new #1 album on the Billboard 200 Music Chart is **"tp-z.com"** by R. Kelly replacing **"The Dynasty Roc La Familia (2000-)"** by Jay-Z..

26
Florida Secretary of State, **Katherine Harris** declares George W. Bush the winner of Florida's 25 electoral votes.

The British Columbia Lions win the 88th **Grey Cup**, with a 28-26 victory over the Montreal Alouettes, at McMahon Stadium in Calgary. B.C. Running-back Robert Drummond is selected as the game's MVP.

27
Canadian Prime Minister, **Jean Chrétien** and his Liberal Party, win a third straight majority as the Canadian elections go off without any problems.

The #1 song on the Billboard Hot Country Singles Music Chart is **"Just Another Day in Paradise"** by Phil Vassar.

British novelist **Sir Malcolm Bradbury**, 68, dies.

28
Geoffrey Rush stars as the "Marquis de Sade" in the film **"Quills"**, directed by Philip Kaufman. The film, released by Searchlight Pictures, co-stars Kate Winslet, Joaquin Phoenix and Michael Caine.

Magician **David Blaine** is encased in a 5-ton block of ice in New York City's Times Square. He will remain there for nearly 62 hours.

29
According to a Justice Department report there are now over **1.2 million inmates in state and federal prisons**. In addition there are 600,000 inmates in local jails. No country has a larger prison population than the United States.

TV Programs Tonight on NBC:
8:00 Titans
9:00 West Wing
10:00 Law & Order

30
The Broadway musical (based on the children's books by Dr. Seuss) **"Seussical: The Musical"**, directed by Frank Galati and starring David Shiner, Anthony Blair Hall, Kevin Chamberlain, Alice Playten and Michele Pawk opens at the Richard Rodgers Theater in New York City.

The cast of the new TV show "Normal, Ohio". (See November 1st)

Geoffrey Rush stars in the new film "Quills". (See November 28th)

Drew Barrymore, Cameron Diaz and Lucy Liu star in the new action-packed film "Charlie's Angels". (See November 3rd)

Jim Carrey stars in the new film "Dr. Seuss' How The Grinch Stole Christmas".

Sunday	Monday	Tuesday	Wednesday	Thursday	Friday	Saturday

Tuesday (top):
Lena Olin and Juliette Binoche star in the new film "Chocolat". (See December 25th)

Zhang Ziyi and Chow Yun Fat star in the new action film "Crouching Tiger, Hidden Dragon". (See December 12th)

Thursday 1:
28 years after the deadliest prison riot in U.S. history left 32 inmates and 11 prison employees dead at **Attica**, officials send out $8-million in settlement checks to 502 Attica inmates or their surviving relatives. All but four of the deaths occurred when state police retook the prison.

Newly-elected Mexican President **Vicente Fox** is sworn into office. **1**

Saturday 2:
Laura Linney and Mark Ruffalo star as reunited siblings "Sammy" & "Terry" in the new film "You Can Count On Me", with Matthew Broderick and Rory Culkin. Writer Kenneth Lonergan directs the movie.

The #1 song on the Billboard Hot Country Singles Music Chart is "We Danced" by Brad Paisley. **2**

Sunday 3:
The world's largest solar wings are installed on the **International Space Station** "Alpha", by two space-walking astronauts. The $600-million U.S. wings span 240 feet from tip to tip and 38 feet across.

Australia wins the inaugural Women's Golf World Cup in Kuala Lumpur, Malaysia. **3**

Monday 4:
French and Kenyan scientists announce that they have found the fossilized remains of mankind's earliest-known ancestor, dubbed "**Millennium Man**", in the Jugen Hills of Kenya's Baringo District. The remains, at least 6 million years old, are more than 1.5 million years older than the previously oldest remains found at Aramis in Ethiopia. **4**

Tuesday 5:
Sisqo, with his hit "The Thong Song", is the big winner at the **Billboard Awards** in Las Vegas, taking home six honors, including *Male Artist of the Year*. The R&B female trio "Destiny's Child" wins four awards, including *Artist and Group of the Year*. 'N Sync and the Dixie Chicks also win four trophies apiece. **5**

Wednesday 6:
Rock 'n roll diva **Tina Turner**, 61, plays the final show of her farewell tour to 18,000 fans at the Arrowhead Pond in Anaheim, California.

TV Programs Tonight on ABC:
9:00 Drew Carey
9:30 Spin City
10:00 Gideon's Crossing **6**

Thursday 7:
It's official, the registrars office in Dornoch, Scotland publishes the intended marriage of **Guy Stewart Richie and Madonna Louise Ciccone**. The marriage is planned to take place on December 22nd at the 776 year-old Dornoch Cathedral in northern Scotland.

FOX-TV premieres "**The Ultimate Auction**", hosted by Sarah Ferguson. **7**

Friday 8:
Pittsburgh Penguins part-owner, **Mario Lemieux**, 35, announces that he will return to playing in the National Hockey League ending 3 1/2 years in retirement.

The film "Proof Of Life" is released starring Meg Ryan as a woman whose husband is kidnapped for ransom in South America. Russell Crowe stars as a hostage negotiator. **8**

Saturday 9:
Quarterback Chris Weinke, 28, of Florida State is named as the 66th **Heisman Trophy** winner. Weinke edges Oklahoma QB Josh Heupel as the college football *Player of the Year*. Weinke is the oldest player ever to win the award.

Canadian Courtney Solomon directs the fantasy feature film based on the game "**Dungeons & Dragons**". Jeremy Irons and Marlon Wayans star in the Alliance Atlantis film. **9**

Sunday 10:
The U.S. golfing pair of Tiger Woods and David Duval win the **World Cup of Golf** in Bella Vista, Argentina. They finish 3 up on Argentina's Eduardo Romero and Angel Carbera. **10**

Monday 11:
Major League Baseball free agent **Alex Rodriguez**, 25, nicknamed "A-Rod", signs the richest contract in sports history with the Texas Rangers. His new contract is worth at least $252 million U.S. over 10 years.

The #1 song on the Billboard Hot Country Singles Music Chart for the 2nd consecutive week is "We Danced" by Brad Paisley. **11**

Tuesday 12:
Chow Yun Fat and Michelle Yeoh star in the film, "**Crouching Tiger, Hidden Dragon**", directed by Ang Lee. Filmed in China in the Mandarin language (with English subtitles), the romantic martial-arts extravaganza will win four Academy Award Oscars, including *Best Foreign Film, Cinematography, Art Direction,* and *Original Score* for Tan Dun. The film is released by Sony Pictures. **12**

Wednesday 13:
Five weeks after election day, Democratic hopeful **Al Gore concedes** the 43rd Presidency of the United States to Republican George W. Bush.

Seven heavily-armed inmates (including two murderers) escape from the **Connally Unit State Prison** near Kennedy, Texas. **13**

Thursday 14:
London, England: **President Clinton** along with the First Lady, **Senator Hillary Rodham Clinton** and their daughter Chelsea, tour Buckingham Palace with Queen Elizabeth. The Clinton's also walk through the crowds in High Park during an unscheduled visit. **14**

Friday 15:
14 years after the world's worst nuclear accident on April 26th, 1986, operators shut down the **Chernoble Nuclear Power Plant** in Kiev, Ukraine.

Buena Vista Pictures releases the animated epic "**The Emperor's New Groove**" with the voices of John Goodman as peasant "Pacha" and David Spade as "Cuzco" the Emperor. **15**

Saturday 16:
U.S. President-elect George W. Bush names retired **Gen. Colin Powell** as his new Secretary of State.

The world's longest-running play, "**The Mousetrap**" by Agatha Christie, celebrates its 20,000th performance in London. The play first opened on November 25th, 1952. It has been translated into 23 languages and seen in more than 40 countries. **16**

Sunday 17:
Mel Gibson knows "**What Women Want**" in the Paramount Pictures comedy film co-starring Helen Hunt, Marisa Tomei, Mark Feuerstein, Lauren Holly and Alan Alda.

Chart Toppers:
The #1 song on the Billboard Hot 100 Singles Music Chart for the 5th consecutive week is "**Independent Women Part I**" by Destiny's Child. **17**

Monday 18:
Popular singer **Christina Aguilera** celebrates her 20th birthday.

The #1 album on the Billboard 200 Music Chart for the 2nd consecutive week is "**Black & Blue**" by The Backstreet Boys. **18**

Tuesday 19:
One of the hottest selling toys for Christmas is the "**Flick Trix Motocross**". Leading the trend in miniature extreme sports toys, the motocross toy, which retails at $9.99, brings the excitement of real racing to your fingertips allowing your fingers to perform stunts like experienced professionals. **19**

Wednesday 20:
An ounce of **gold** sells for $273. An ounce of **silver** trades at $4.58.

SILVER

The average price of **unleaded gasoline** has now risen to $1.54 per gallon. **20**

Thursday 21:
The **Top-Grossing films** released in the year 2000 were:
1) "Dr. Seuss' How the Grinch Stole Christmas" - $253.4 million
2) "Mission: Impossible 2" - $215.4 million
3) "Gladiator" - $186.7 million
4) "The Perfect Storm" - $182.6 million
5) "Meet the Parents" - $161.3 million

ADMIT ONE **21**

Friday 22:
Pop star **Madonna**, 42, marries director Guy Ritchie, 32, at the Dornoch Cathedral in Scotland. Their 4-month-old son Rocco was baptized yesterday.

20th Century Fox releases the drama film "**Cast Away**", directed by Robert Zemeckis. The film stars Tom Hanks as the sole survivor of a plane crash, alone for years on a tropical island. **22**

Saturday 23:
Comic pianist and conductor, **Victor Borge**, 91, dies in his sleep at home in Greenwich, Connecticut. Borge's one-man Broadway show "Comedy in Music" ran for a record 849 performances in the 1950's.

BROADWAY

Billy Barty, 76, the TV actor who founded the advocacy group for people with dwarfism, "Little People of America", dies in hospital in Glendale, California. **23**

Sunday 24:
The **Best-Selling Books** at this time are:
Fiction Hardback
1) "Roses Are Red" by James Patterson
2) "The Bear and the Dragon" by Tom Clancy

Mass Market Paperbacks
1) "Heart of the Sea" by Nora Roberts
2) "False Memory" by Dean Koontz

General Hardback
1) "The Beatles Anthology" by the Beatles **24**

Monday 25:
Sandra Bullock stars as a beauty queen cop in the new comedy film "**Miss Congeniality**", with Michael Caine, Benjamin Bratt and Candice Bergen. The film is directed by Donald Petrie and released by Warner Bros. Pictures.

Juliette Binoche sets up a chocolaterie in the romantic fantasy film, "**Chocolat**". The film directed by Lasse Hallstrom, co-stars Johnny Depp, Lena Olin, Alfred Molina and Judi Dench. **25**

Tuesday 26:
The Beatles are back as the 1964 Richard Lester film "**A Hard Days Night**" is re-released in theatres across the country. The film features a fully restored picture and digitally restored soundtrack.

Stage and screen star **Jason Robards**, 78, dies in Bridgeport, Connecticut after a long battle with cancer. Robards won *Best Supporting Actor Oscars* in 1976 and 1977 for "All The President's Men" and "Julia". **26**

Wednesday 27:
Mario Lemieux returns to the National Hockey League and assists on a goal just 33 seconds into his comeback. Lemieux plays 20:46 minutes and scores 1 goal and adds 2 assists, as the Penguins down the Toronto Maple Leafs 5-0 in Pittsburgh.

St. Louis Rams running-back **Marshall Faulk** is named as the NFL's *Most Valuable Player*, in a poll conducted by the Associated Press. **27**

Thursday 28:
Steven Soderbergh directs the new film "**Traffic**", based on the 1990 British TV mini-series dealing with the cocaine drug trade. The movie stars Michael Douglas, Catherine Zeta-Jones, Dennis Quaid, Don Cheadle, and Benicio Del Toro, who will win the *Best Supporting Actor* Oscar for his performance as a Mexican cop. The film will win four Oscars in total, including *Adapted Screenplay* for Stephen Gaghan and the *Director Award* for Soderbergh. **28**

Friday 29:
George Clooney and John Turturro star in the Coen Brothers film "**O Brother Where Art Thou?**", with Tim Blake Nelson and John Goodman.

Bruce Greenwood stars as the late president "**John F. Kennedy**" in the movie "**Thirteen Days**". The film, directed by Roger Donaldson, and co-starring Kevin Costner, is a political thriller telling of the days surrounding the Cuban missile crisis. **29**

Saturday 30:
NFL Wild Card Games:
AFC: Miami 23 - Indianapolis 17 (overtime)
NFL: New Orleans 31 - St. Louis 28

The #1 song on the Billboard Hot Country Singles Music Chart for the 3rd consecutive week is "**My Next Thirty Years**" by Tim McGraw. **30**

Sunday 31:
NFL Wild Card Games:
AFC: Baltimore 21 - Denver 3
NFC: Philadelphia 21 - Tampa Bay 3

The estimated **population** in the United States at this time is 281,421,906. **31**

The new film "Traffic" stars Dennis Quaid, Catherine Zeta-Jones, Benico Del Torro, Michael Douglas and Amy Irving. (See December 28th)

Tom Hanks stars in the new film "Cast Away". (See December 22nd)